Viking Swear Word Coloring Book

By: Shazza T. Jones

Introduction

Learn some Viking swear words while you sit back and color the pages.

Table of Contents

Hrafnasueltir: Coward

Hrodi: Snot

Istrumagi: Fat Gut

Kerling: Old Hag

Lodinkinni: Shaggy Hair

Meinfretr: Stinky Fart

Meyla: Act Like A little Girl

Miklimunnr: Loudmouth

Oskilgetinn: Bastard

Skreyja: Incompetent

Tik: Bitch

Vitskertr: Numnut

Ormstunga: Snake Tongue

Dofni: Dopey

Qlfuss: Drunkard

Blatqnn: Blacktooth

Gellir: Screamer

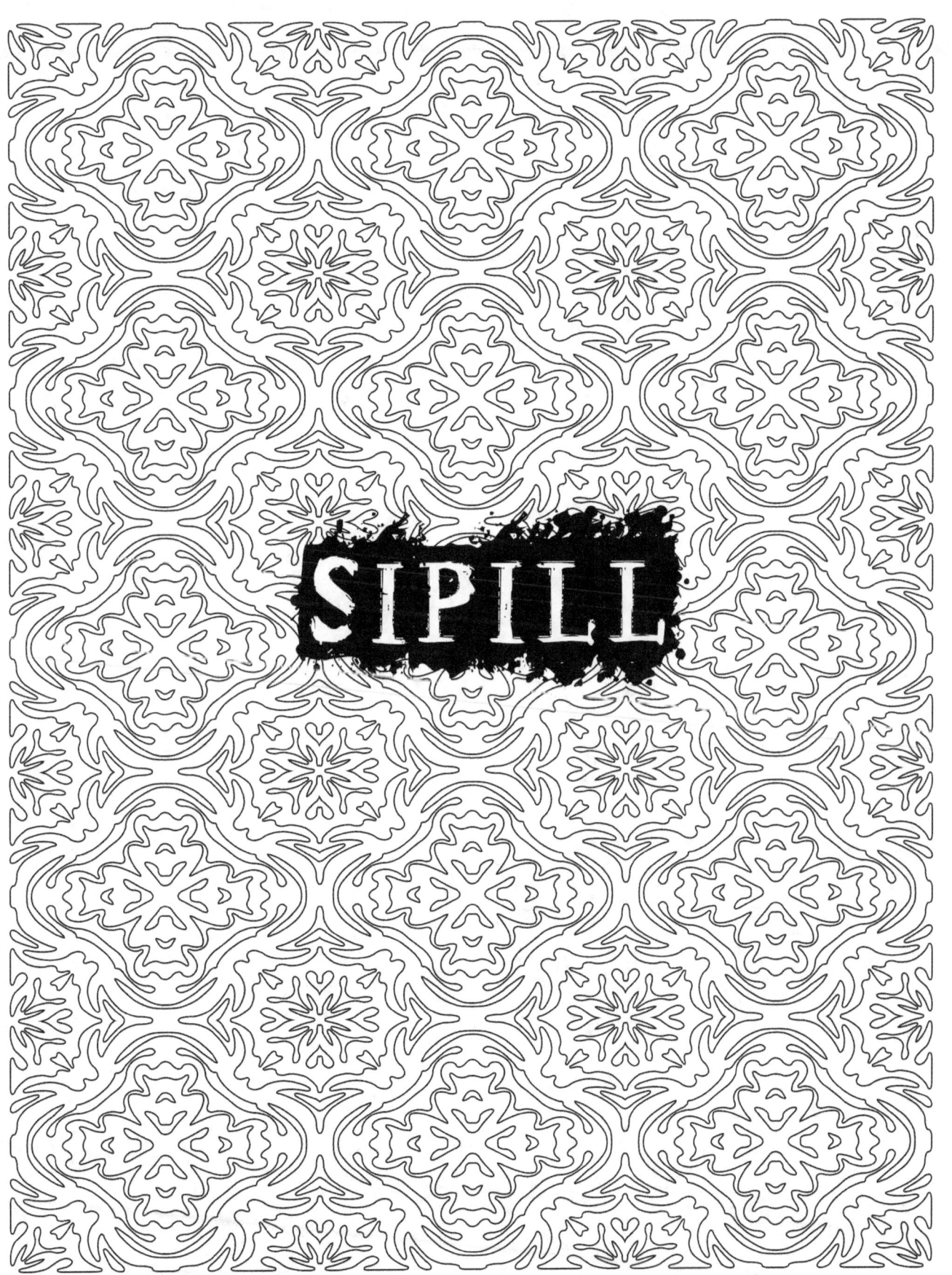

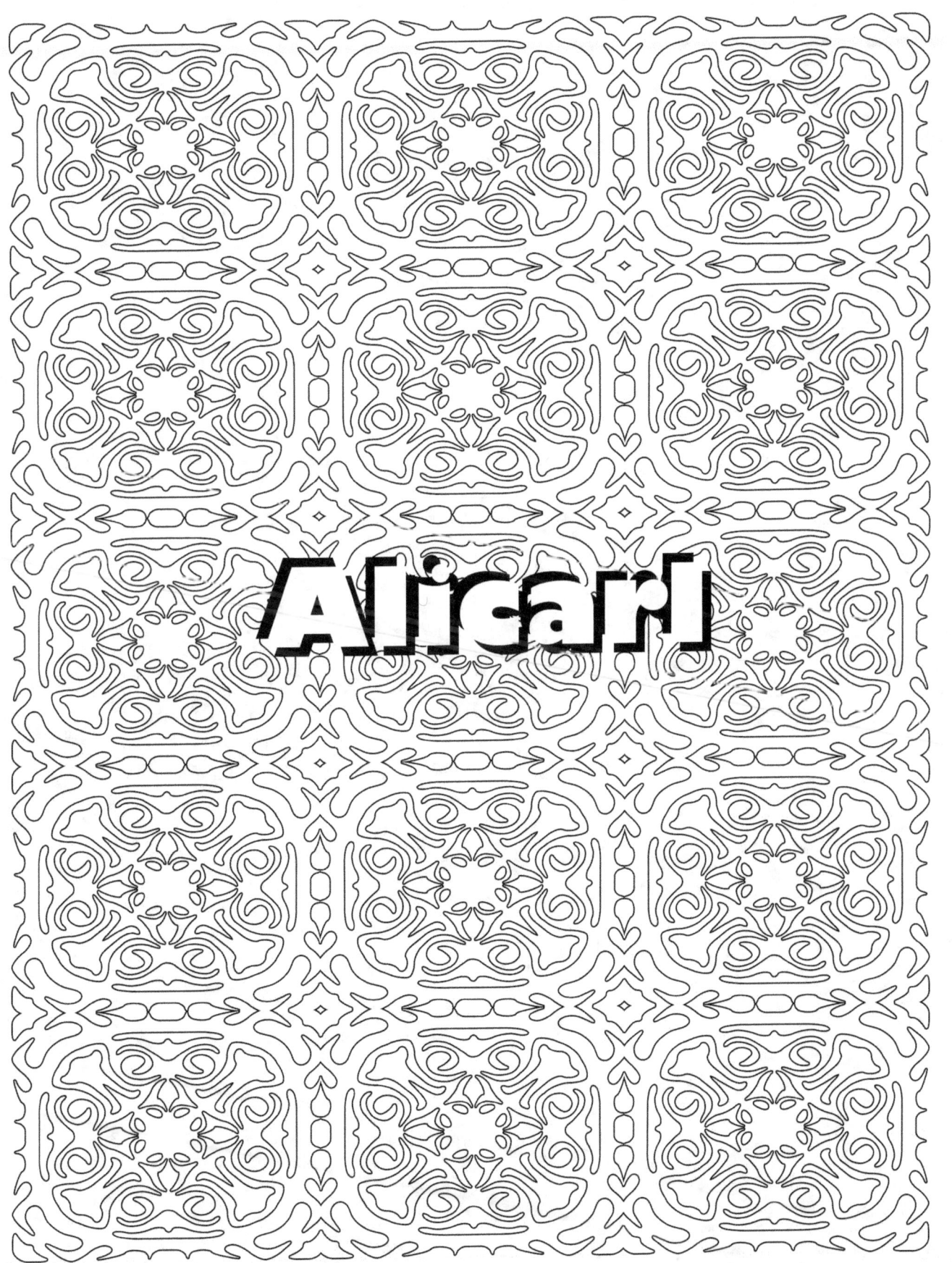

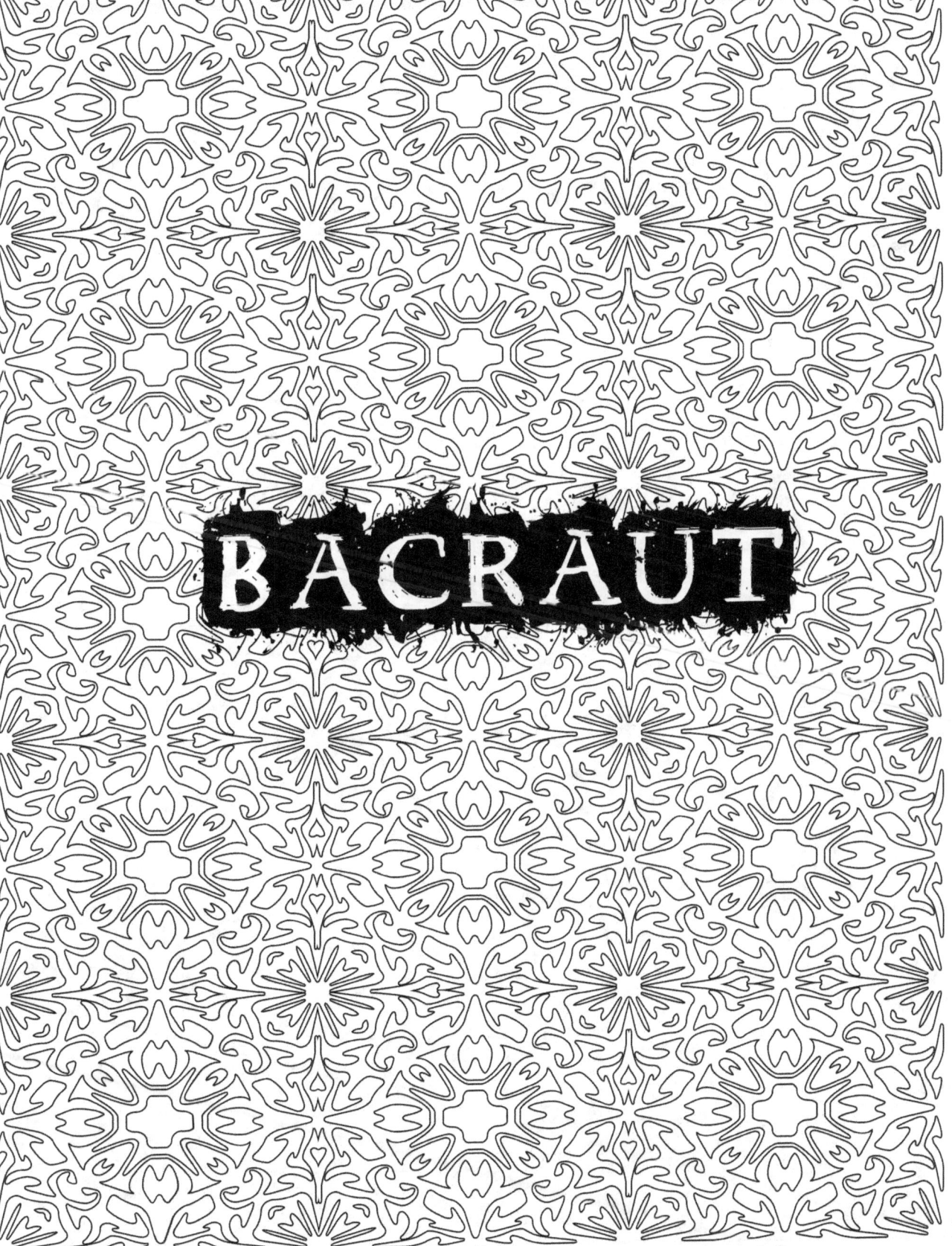

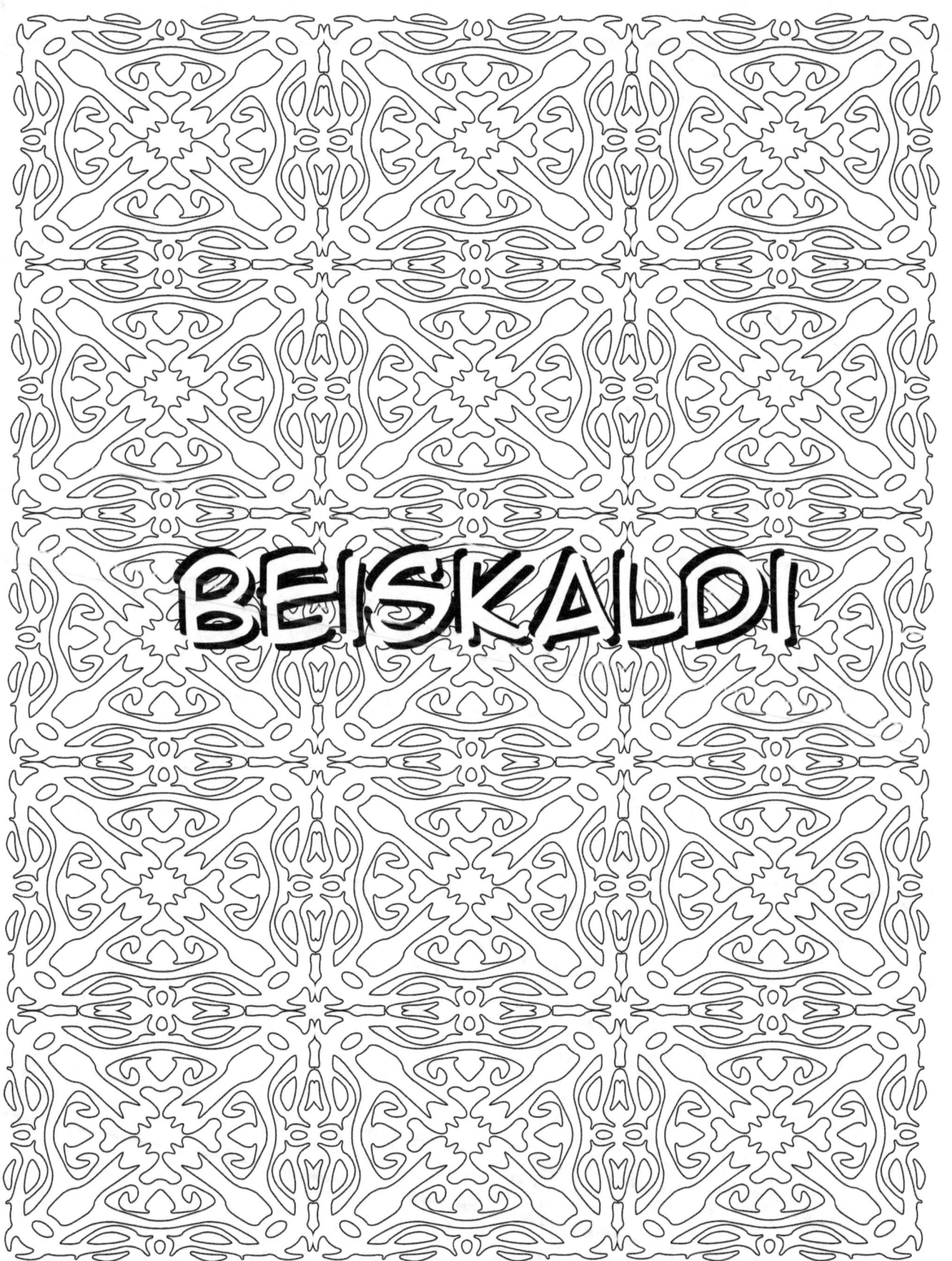

BEISKALDI

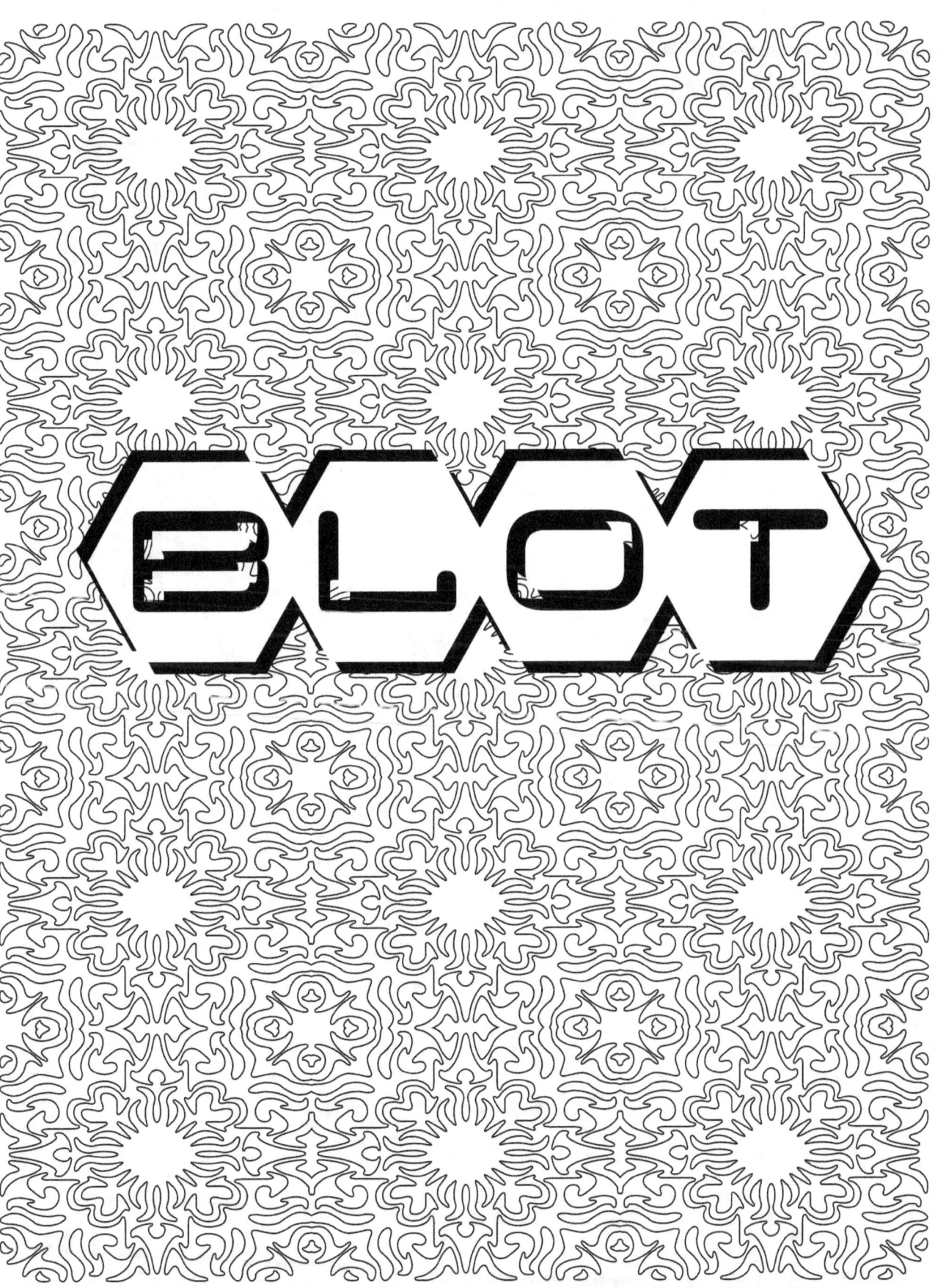

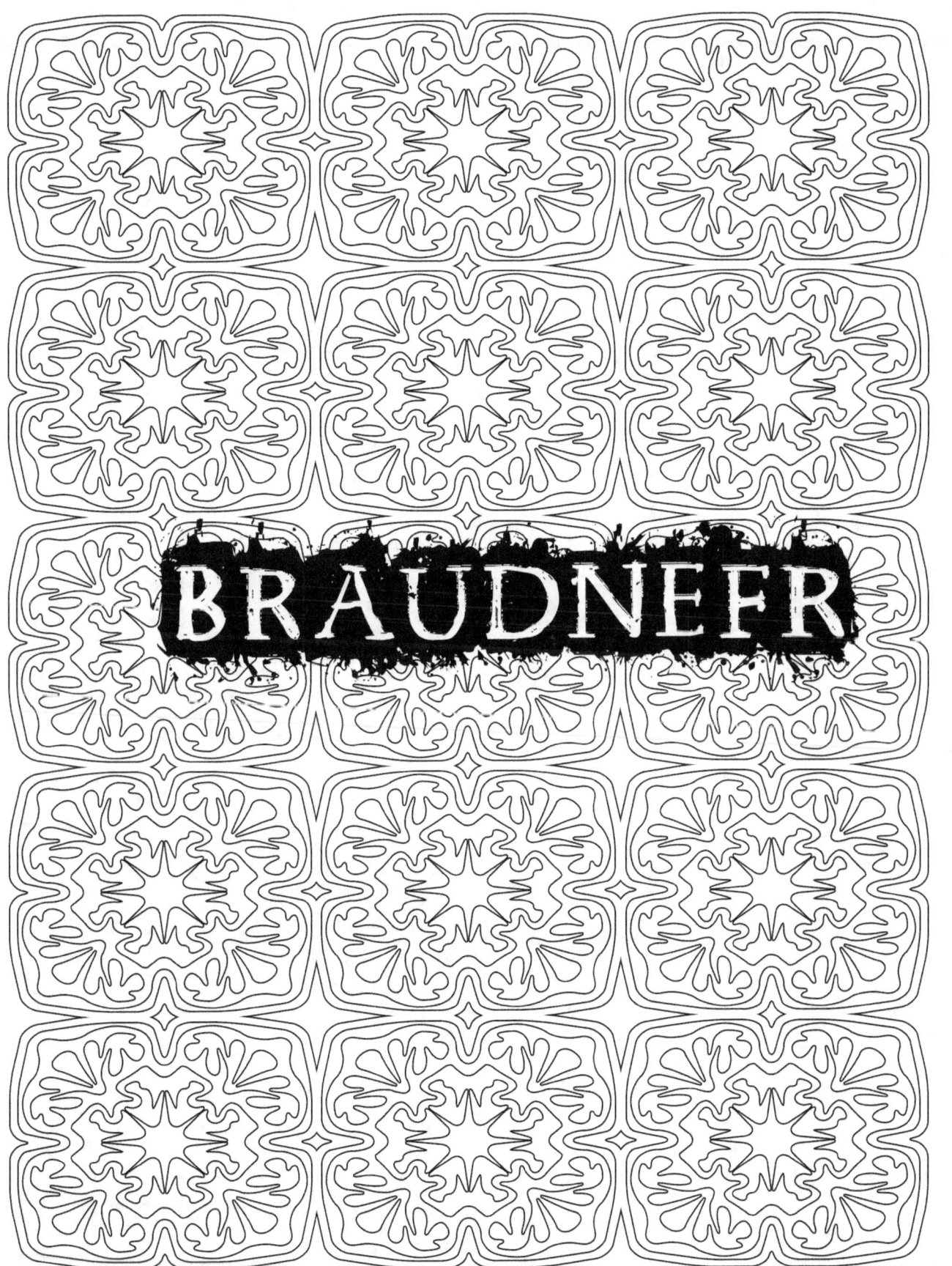

BRAUDNEFR

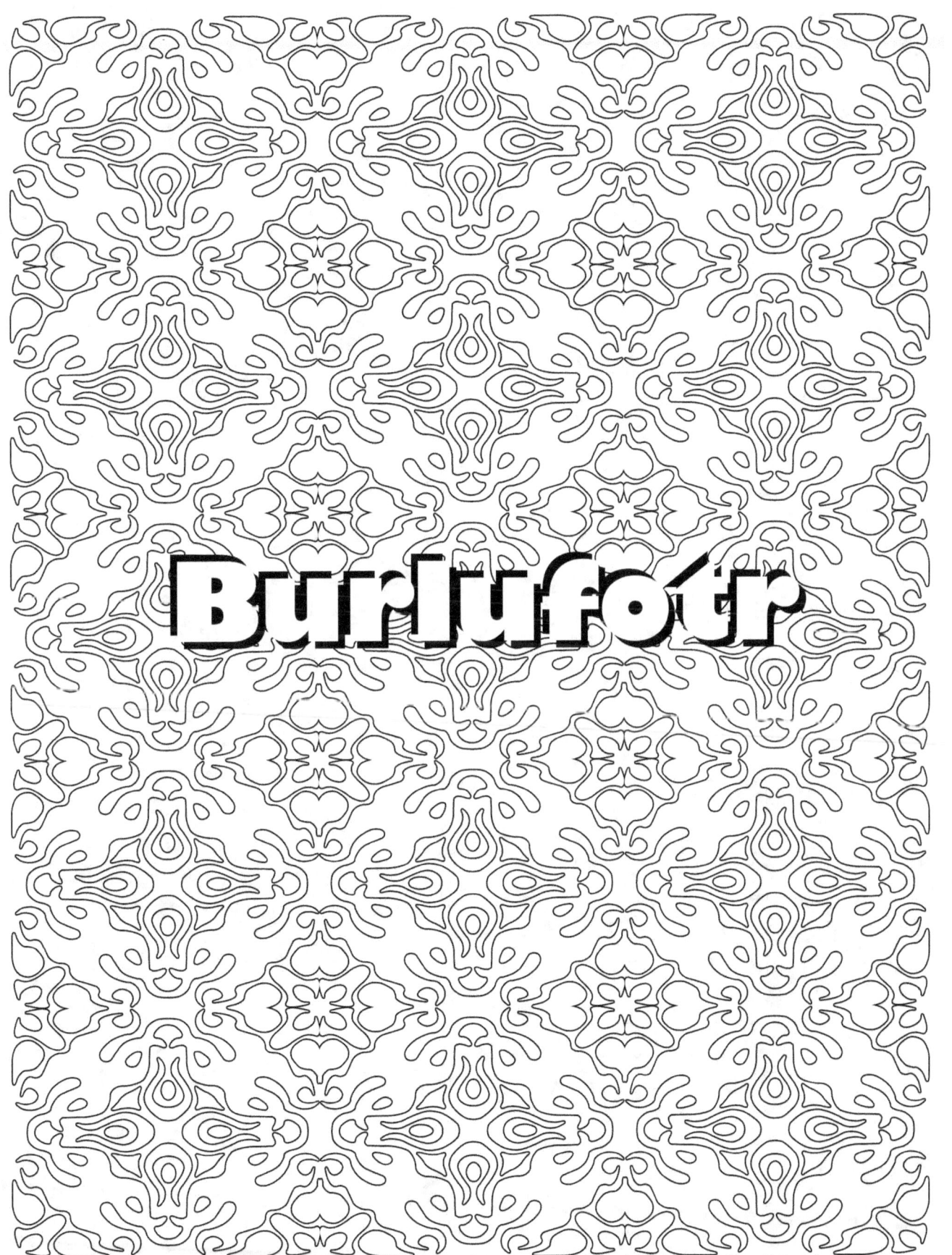

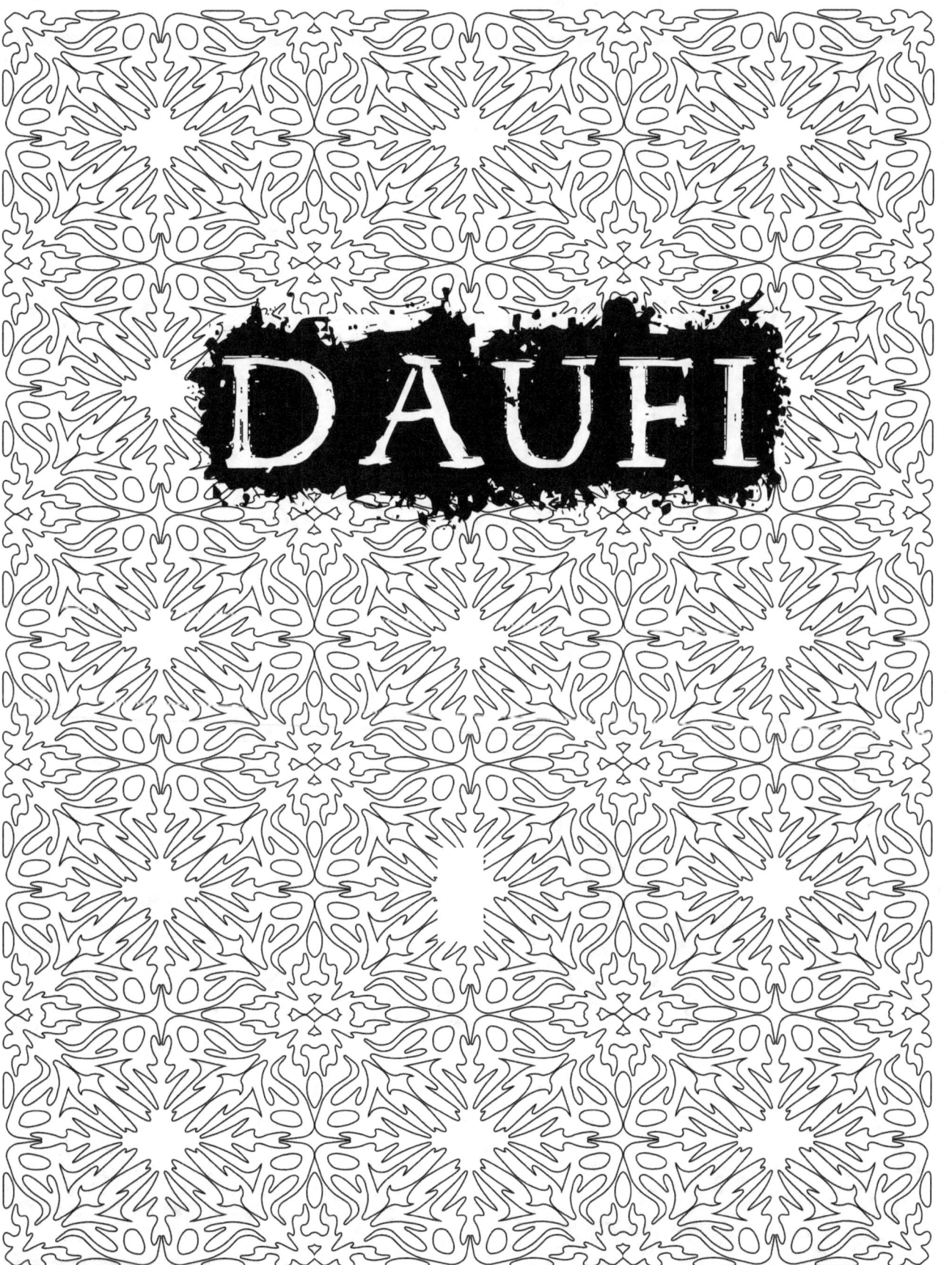

DAUFI

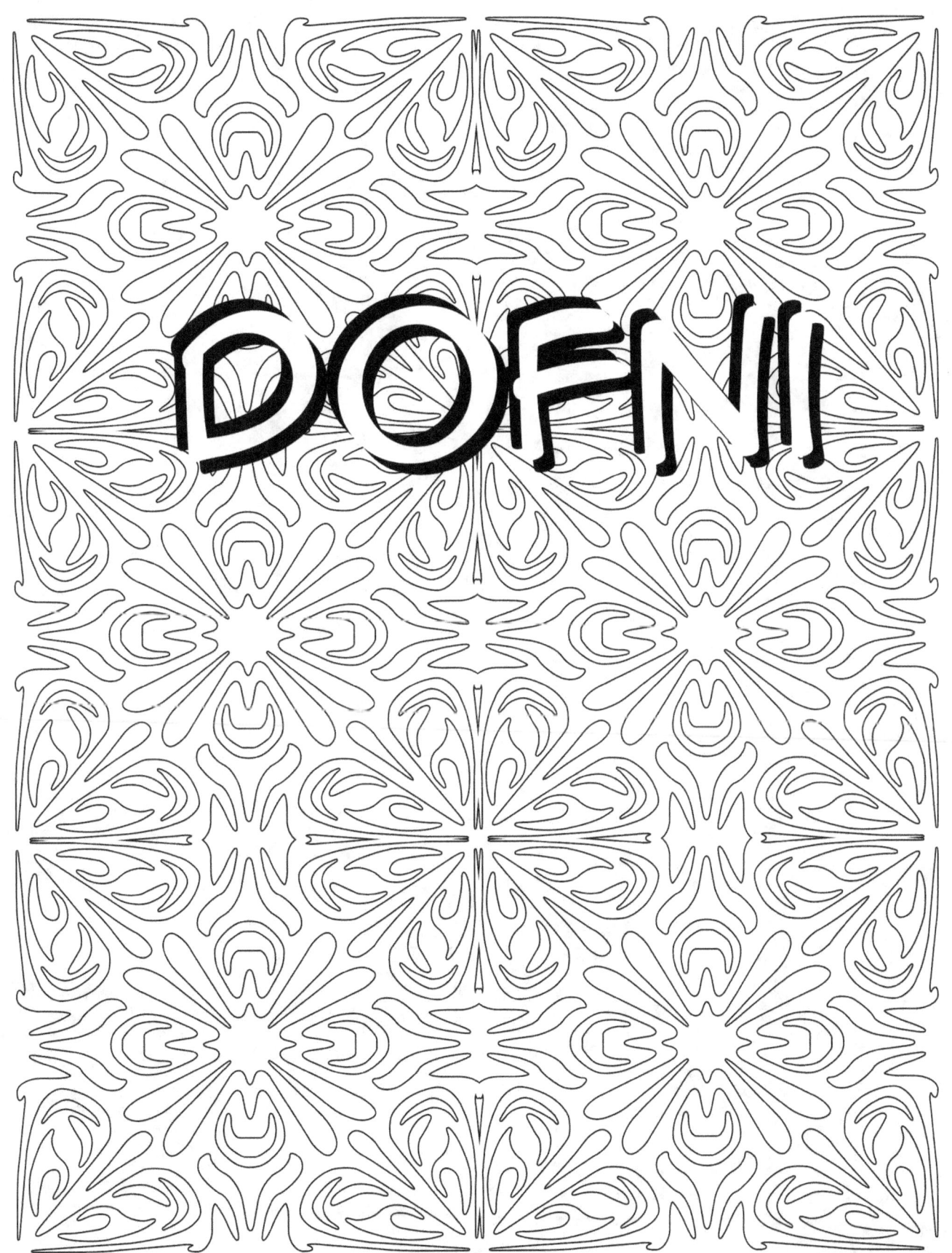

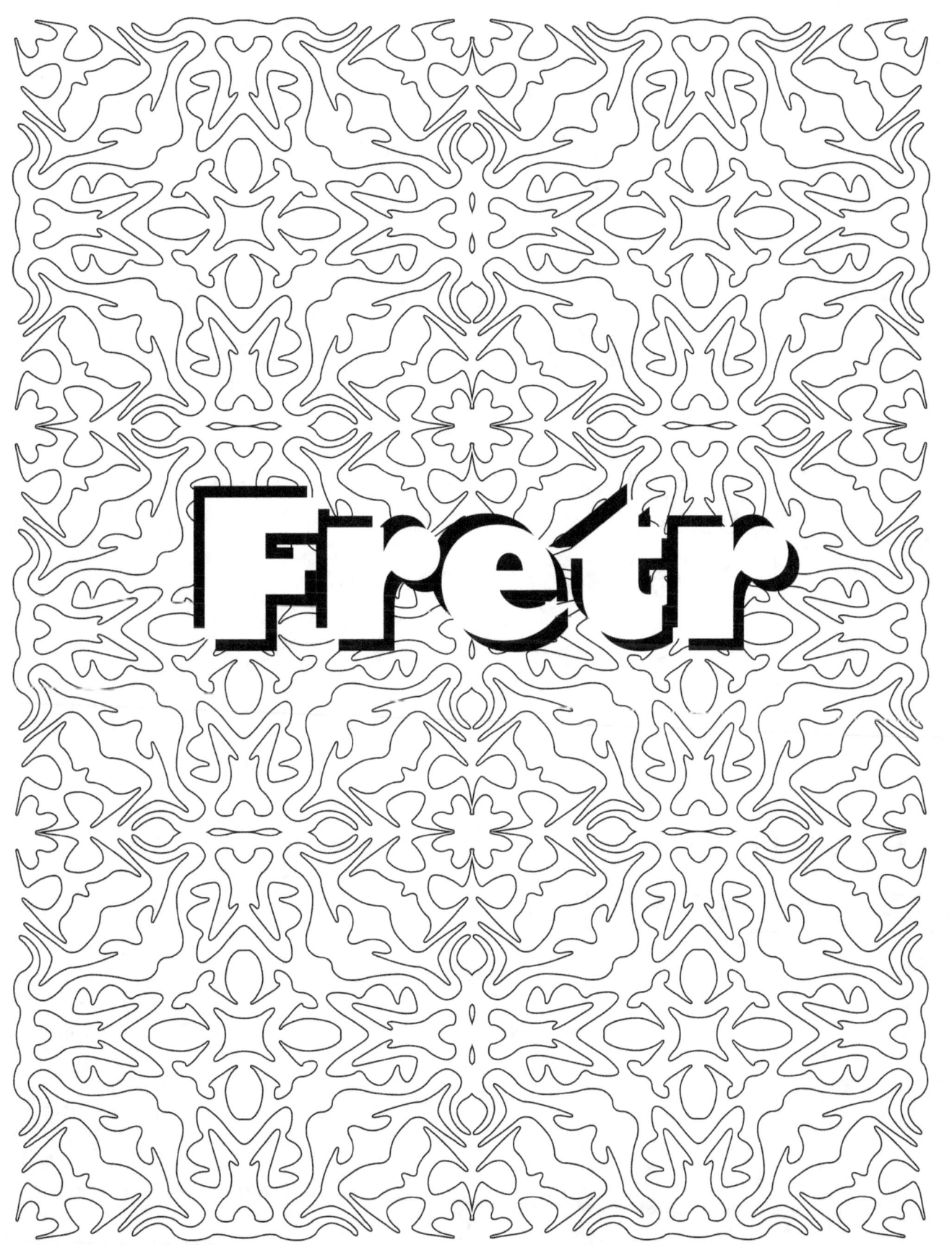

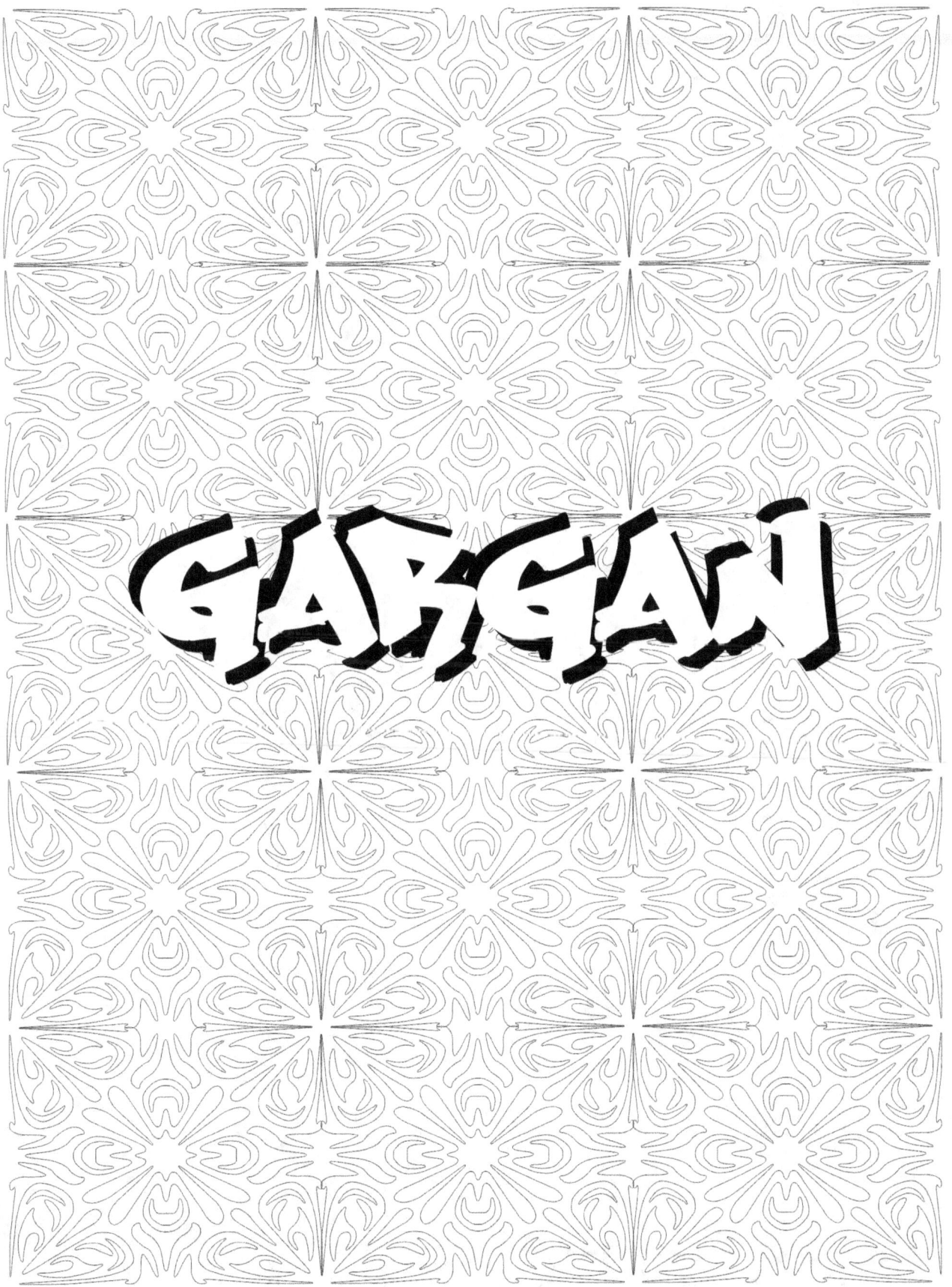

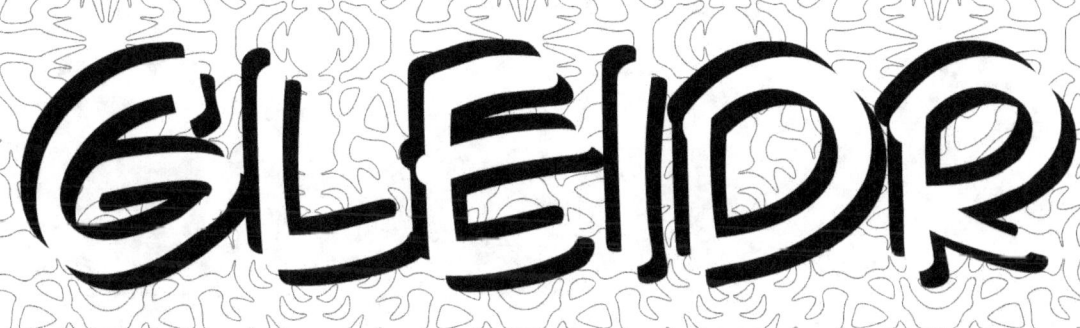

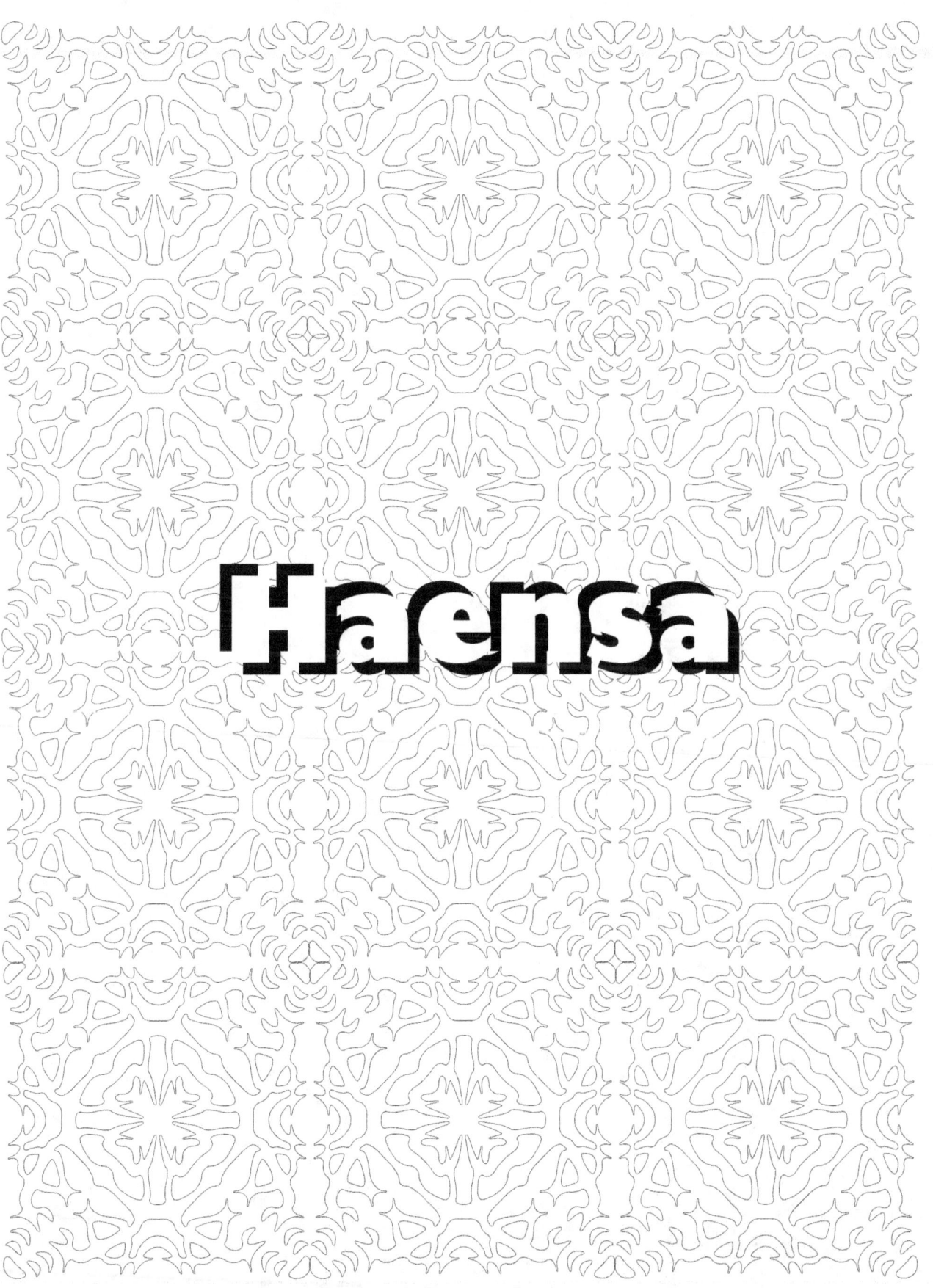

Haensa

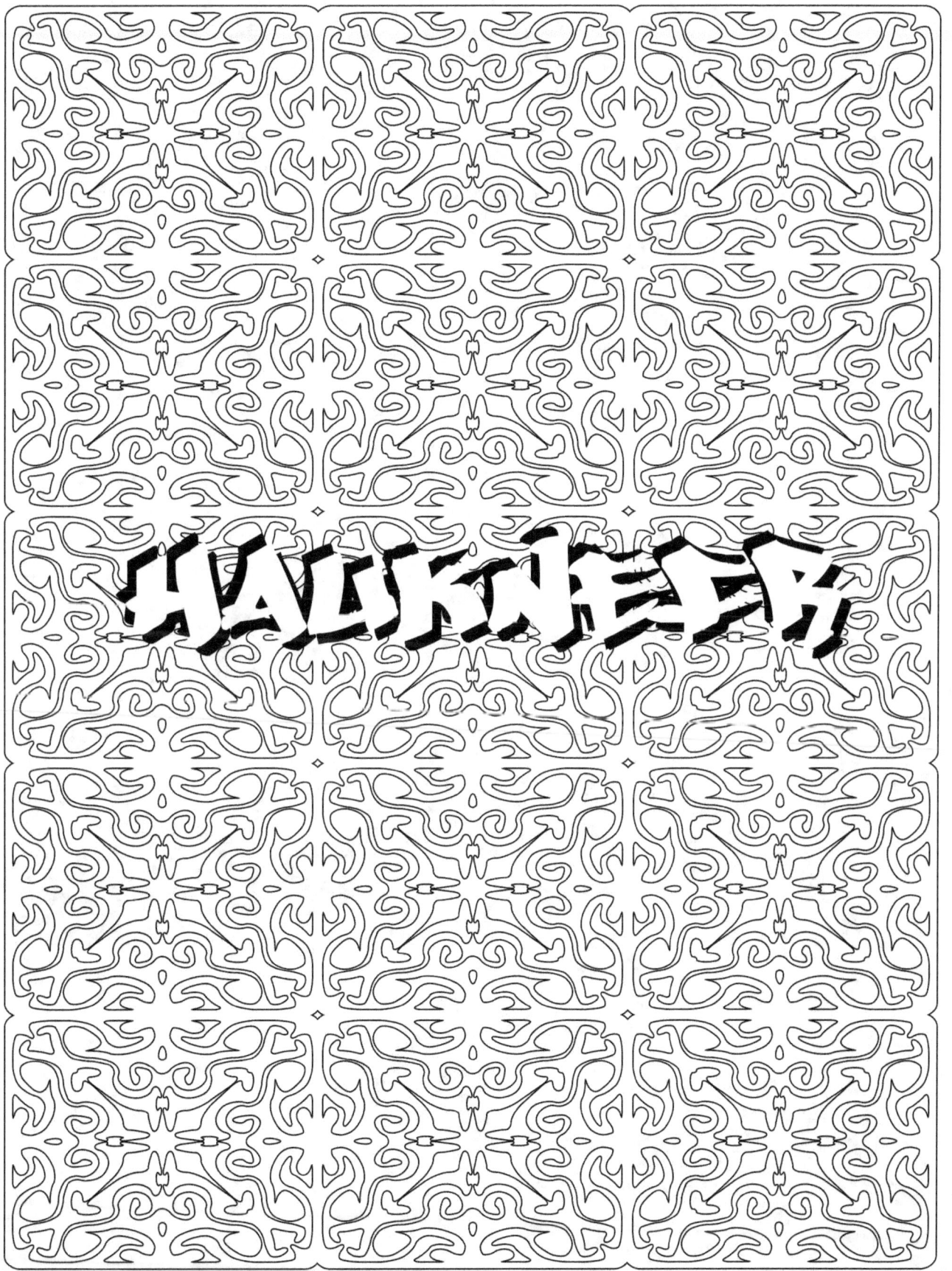

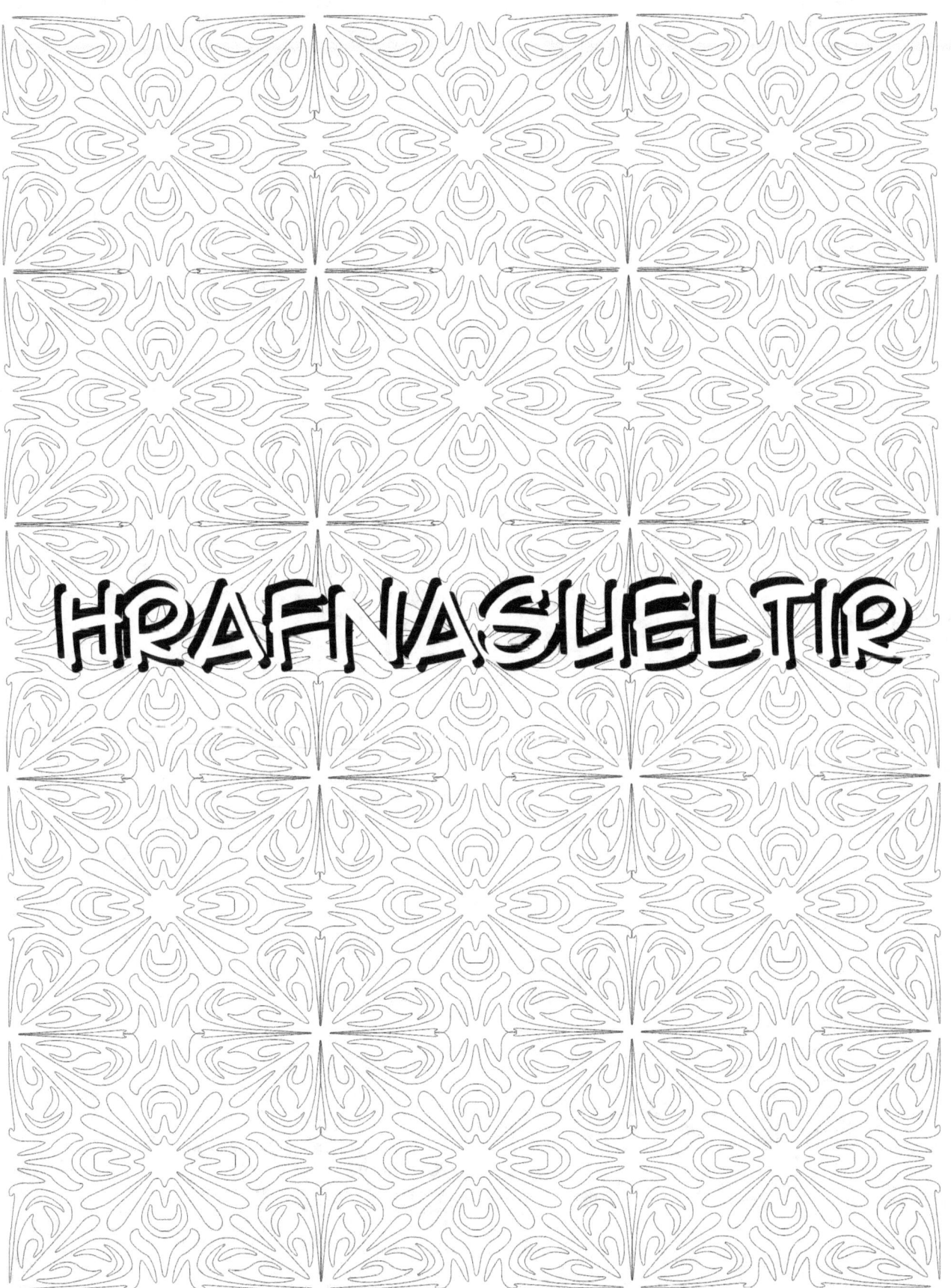

HRAFNASUELTIR

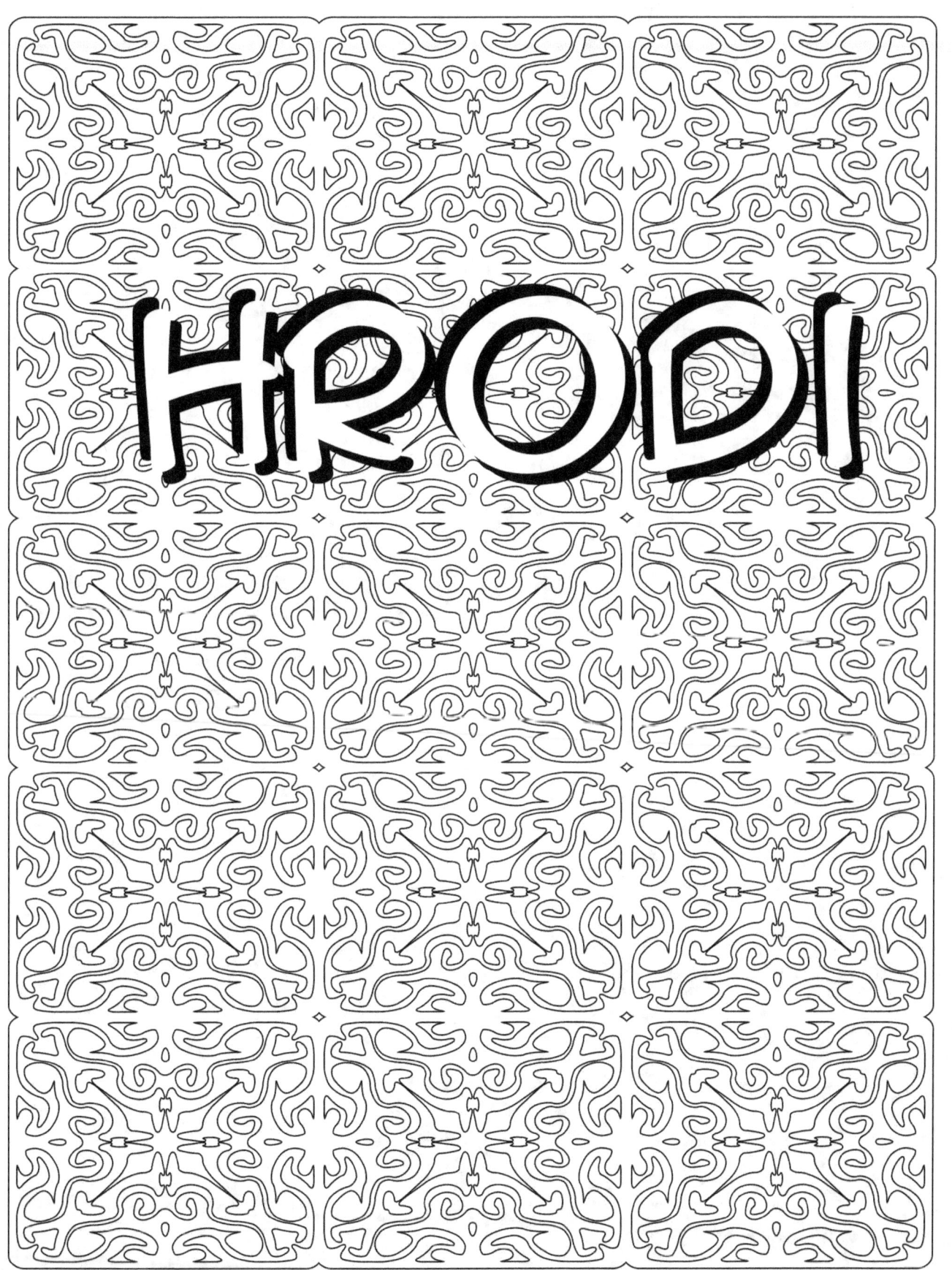

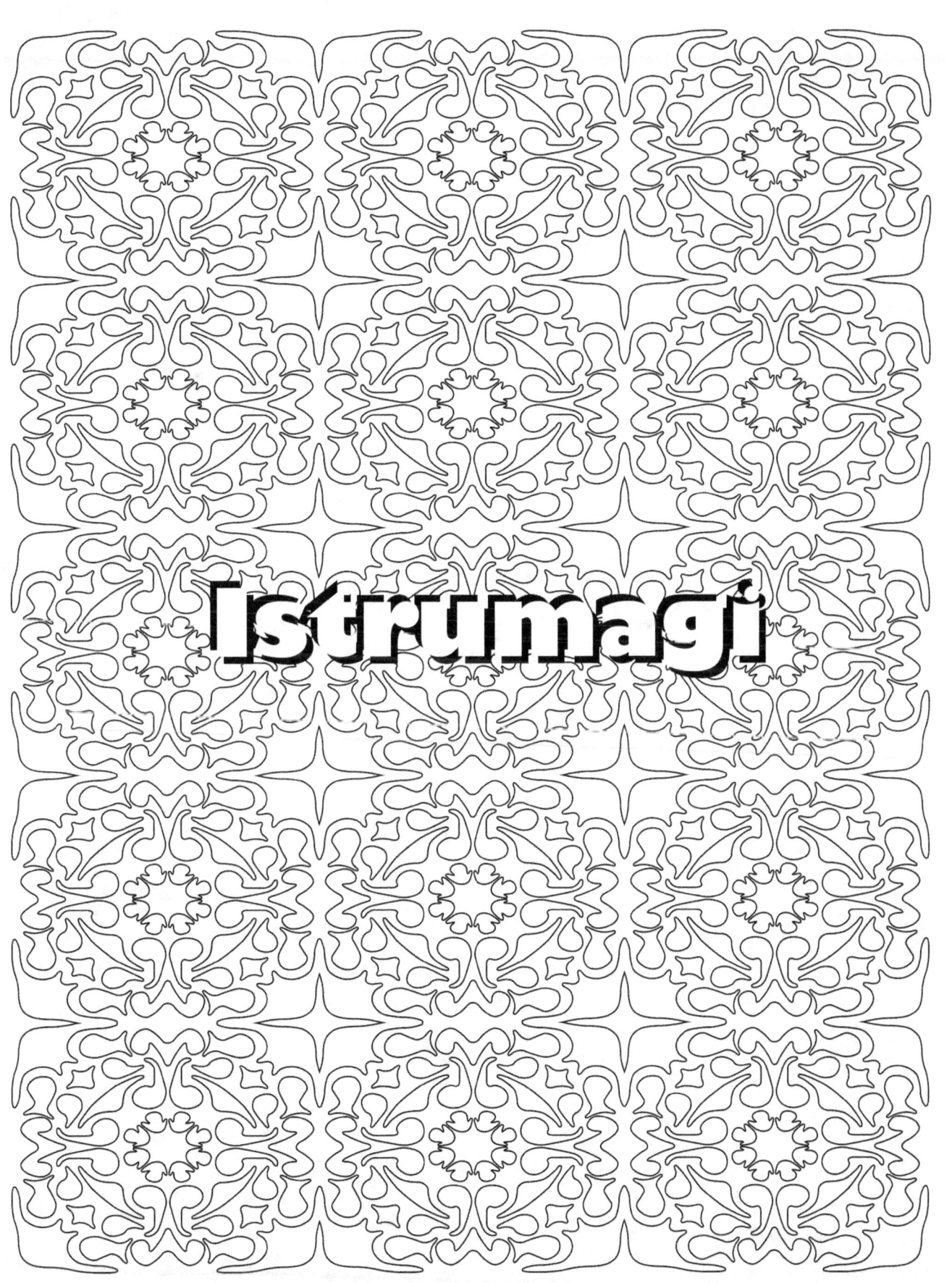

[Istrumagj

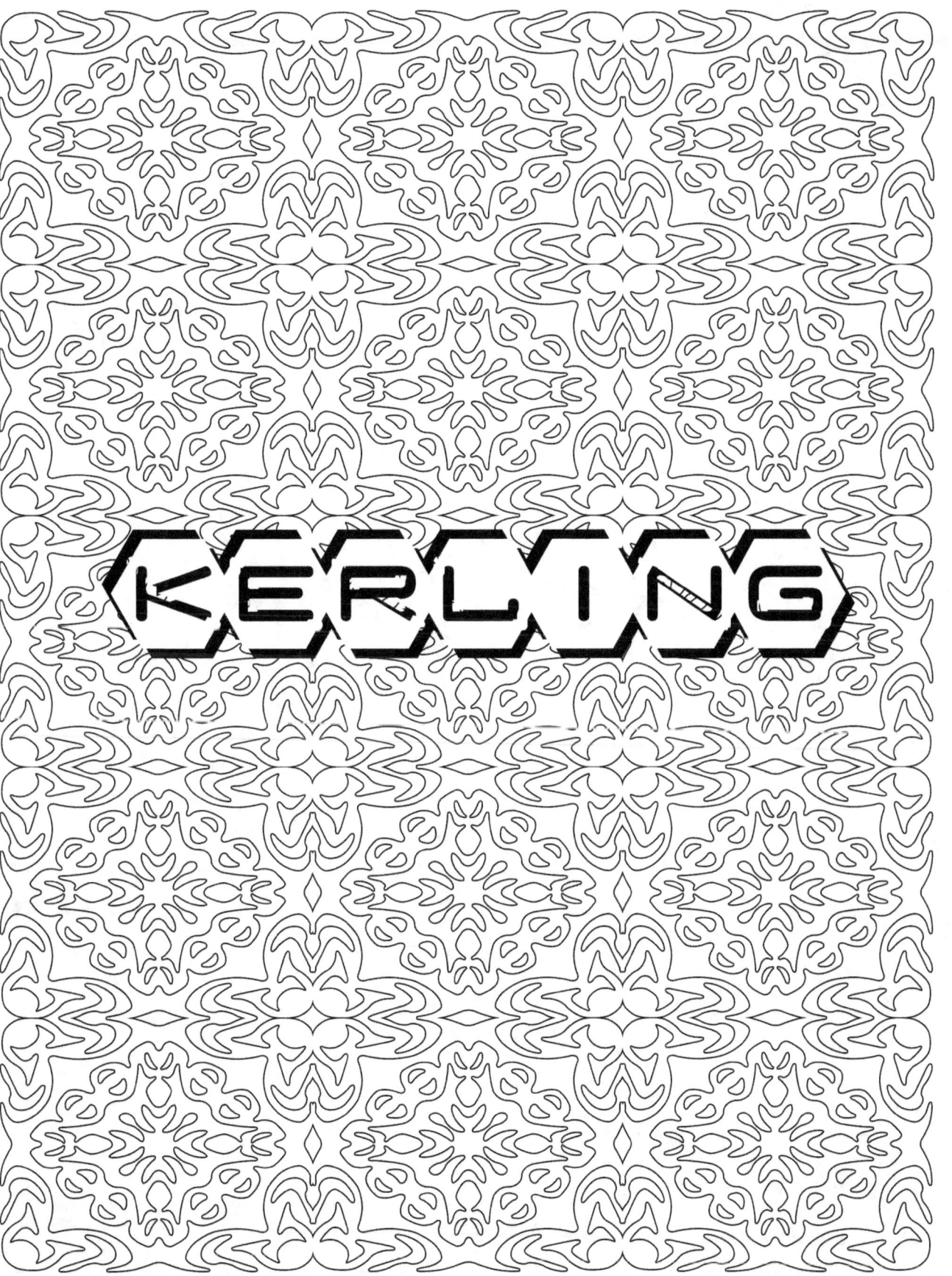

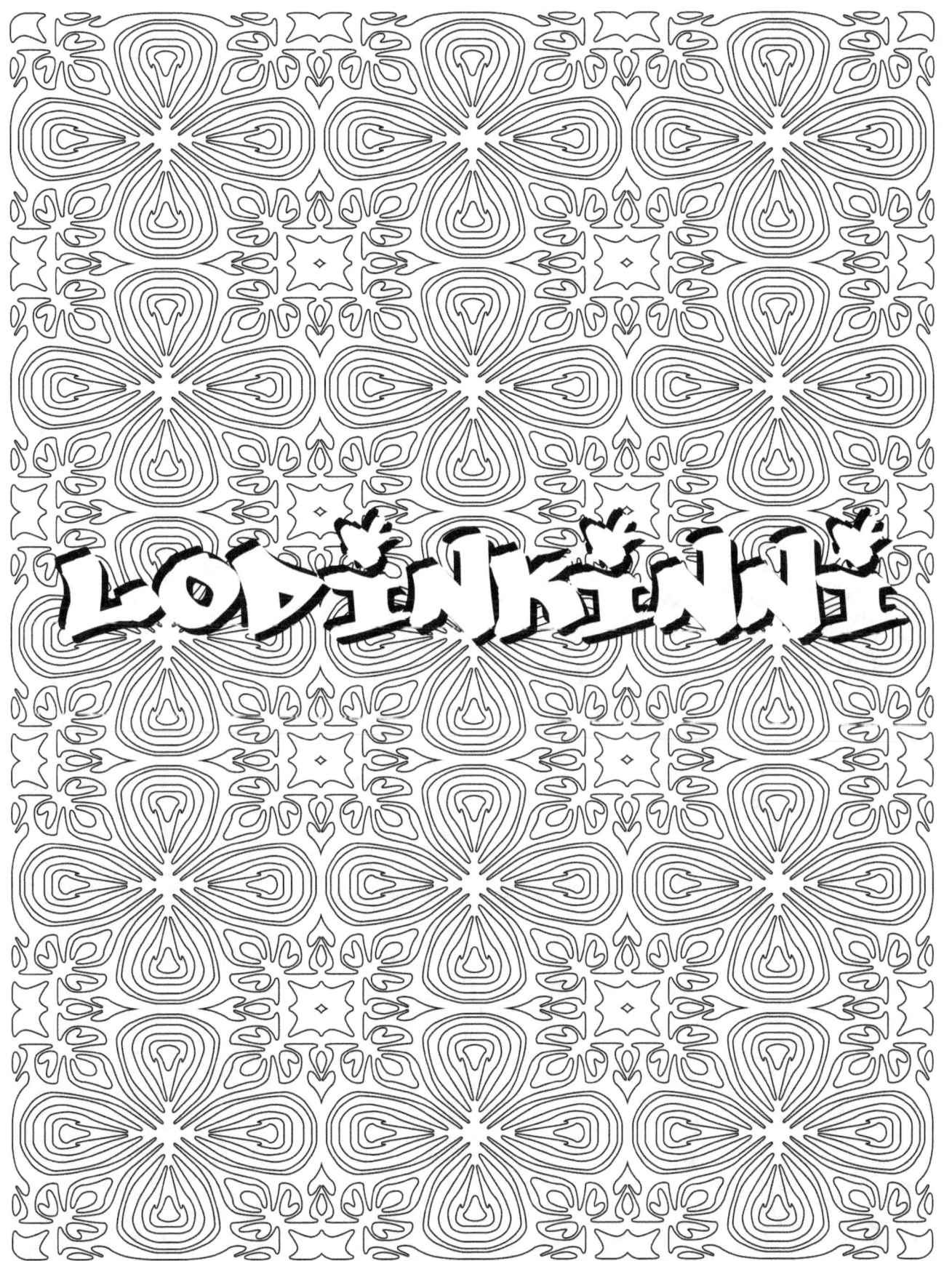

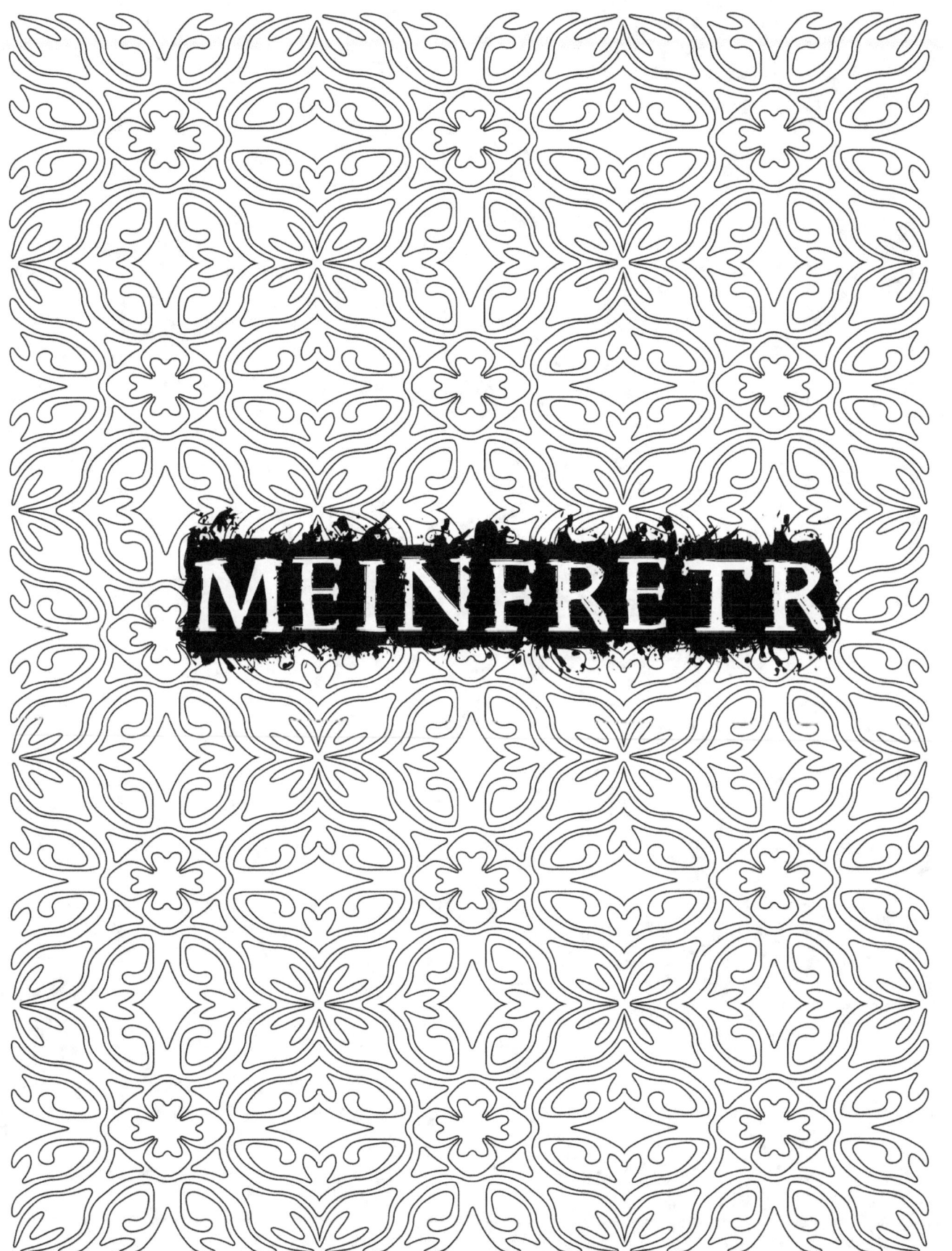

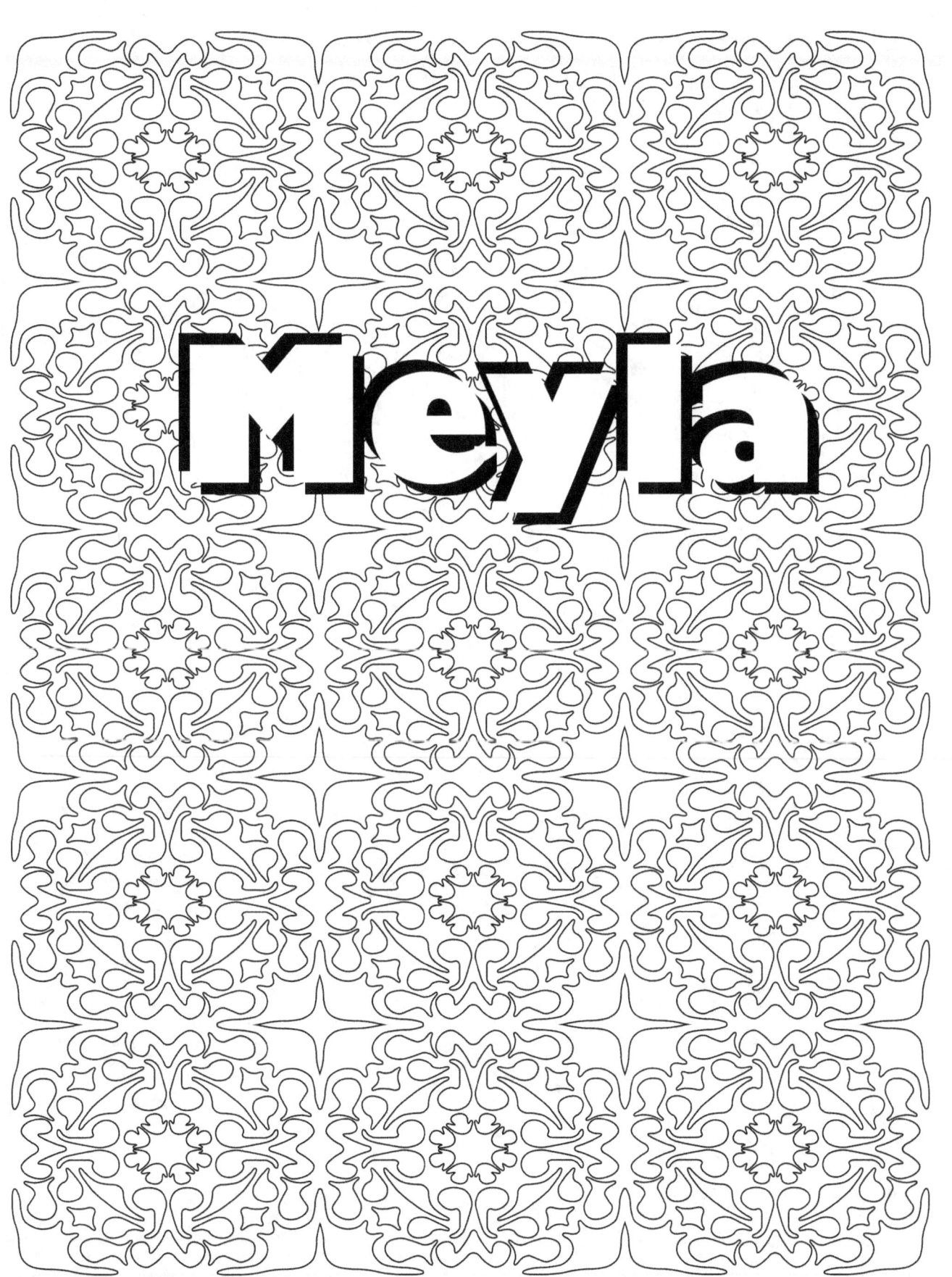

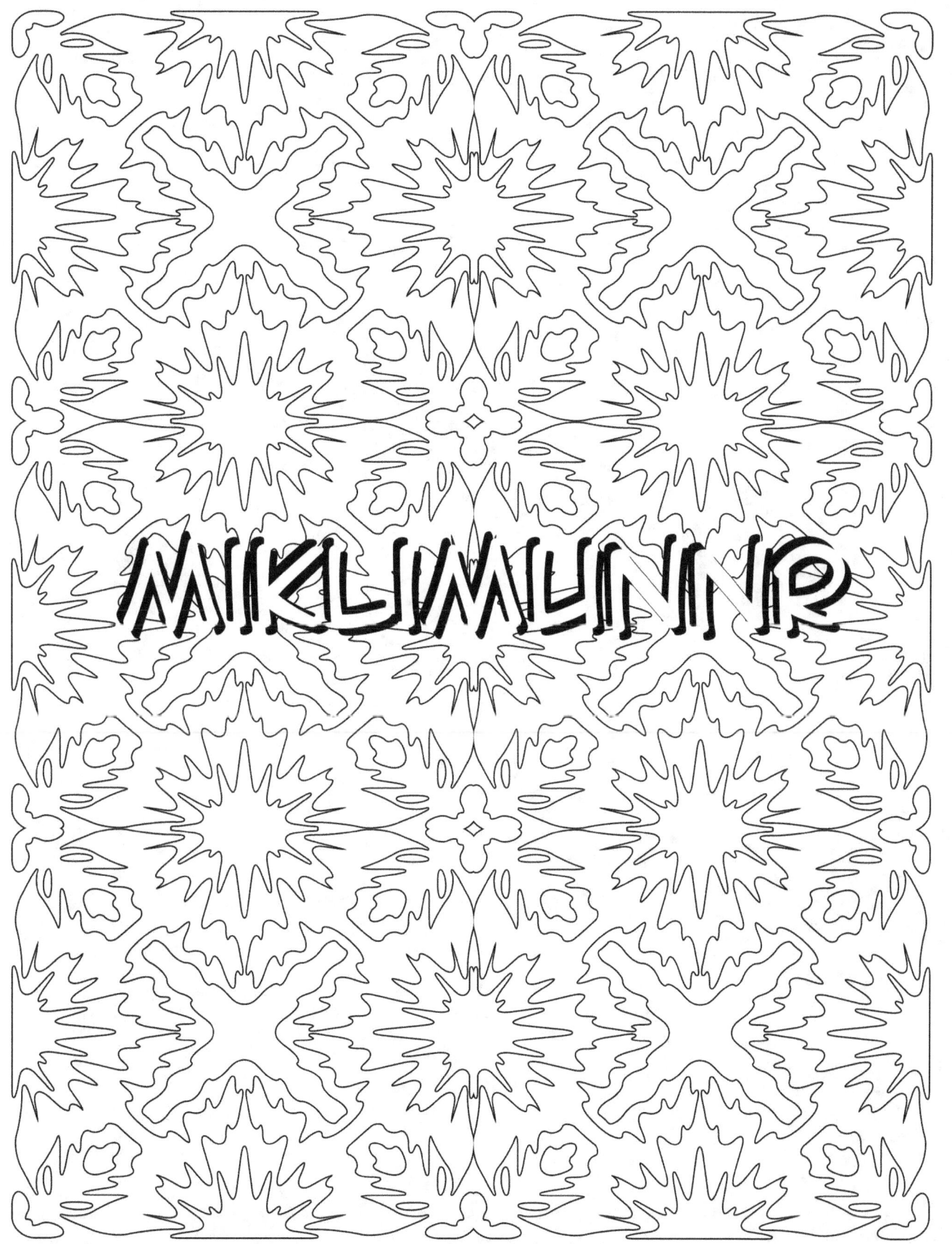

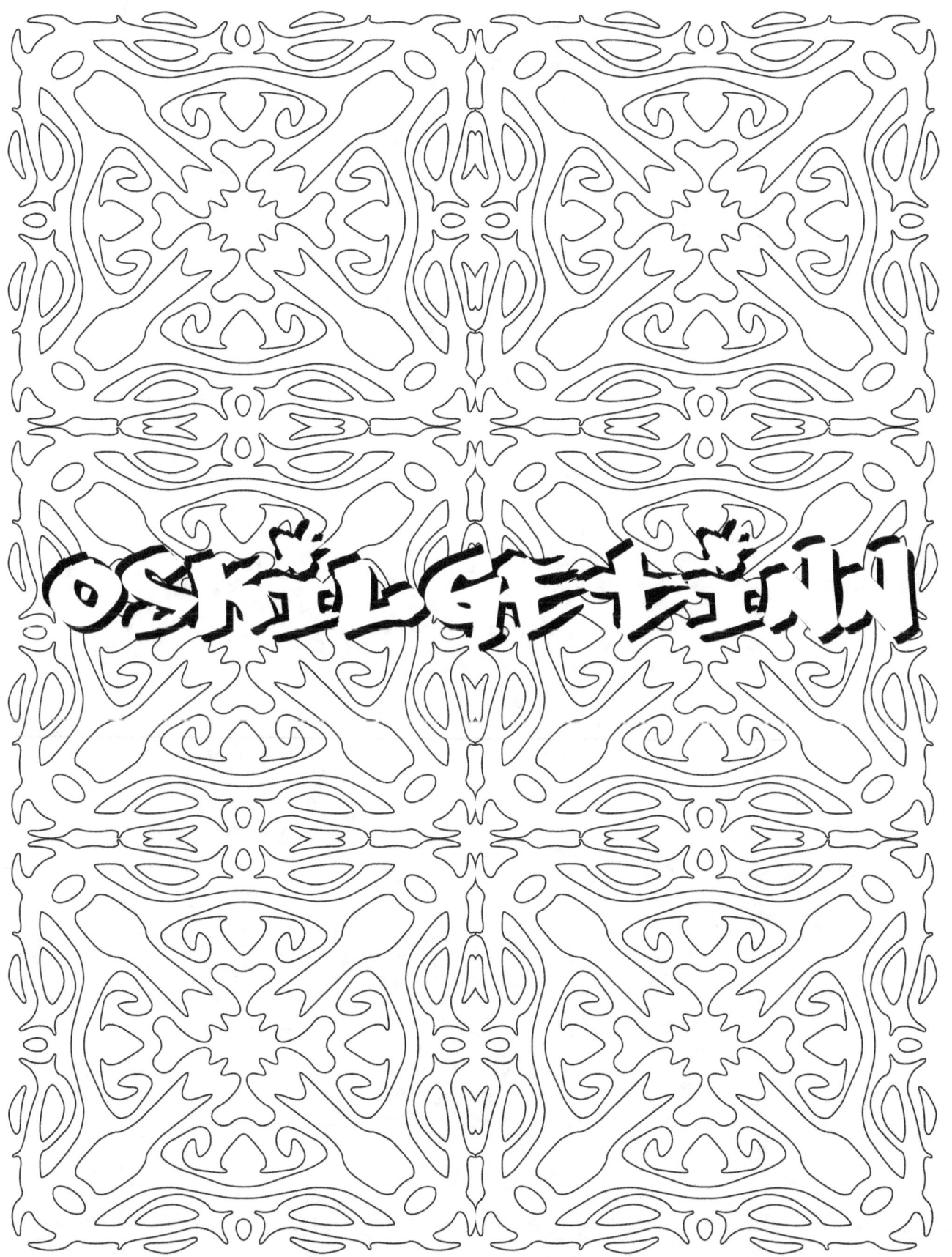

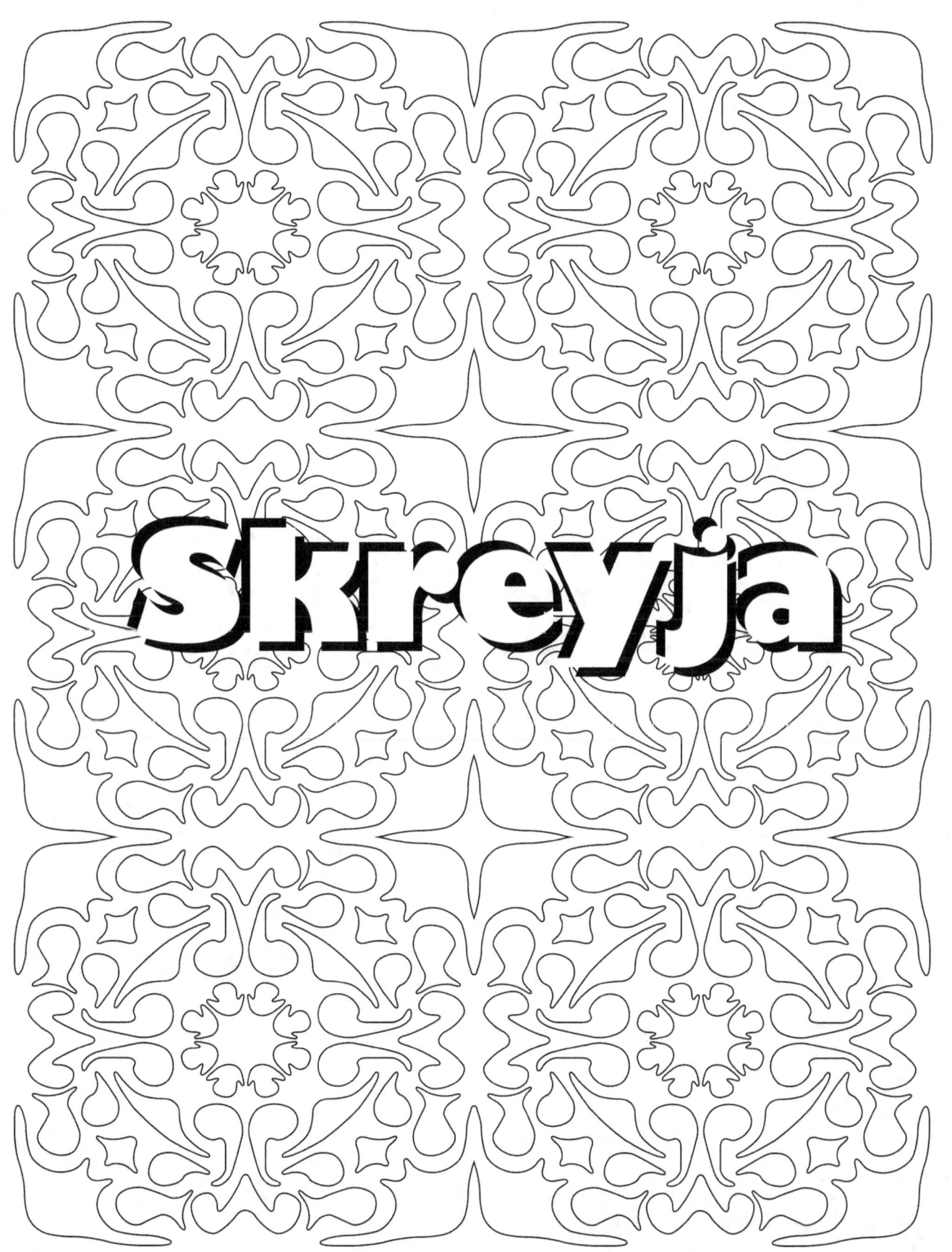

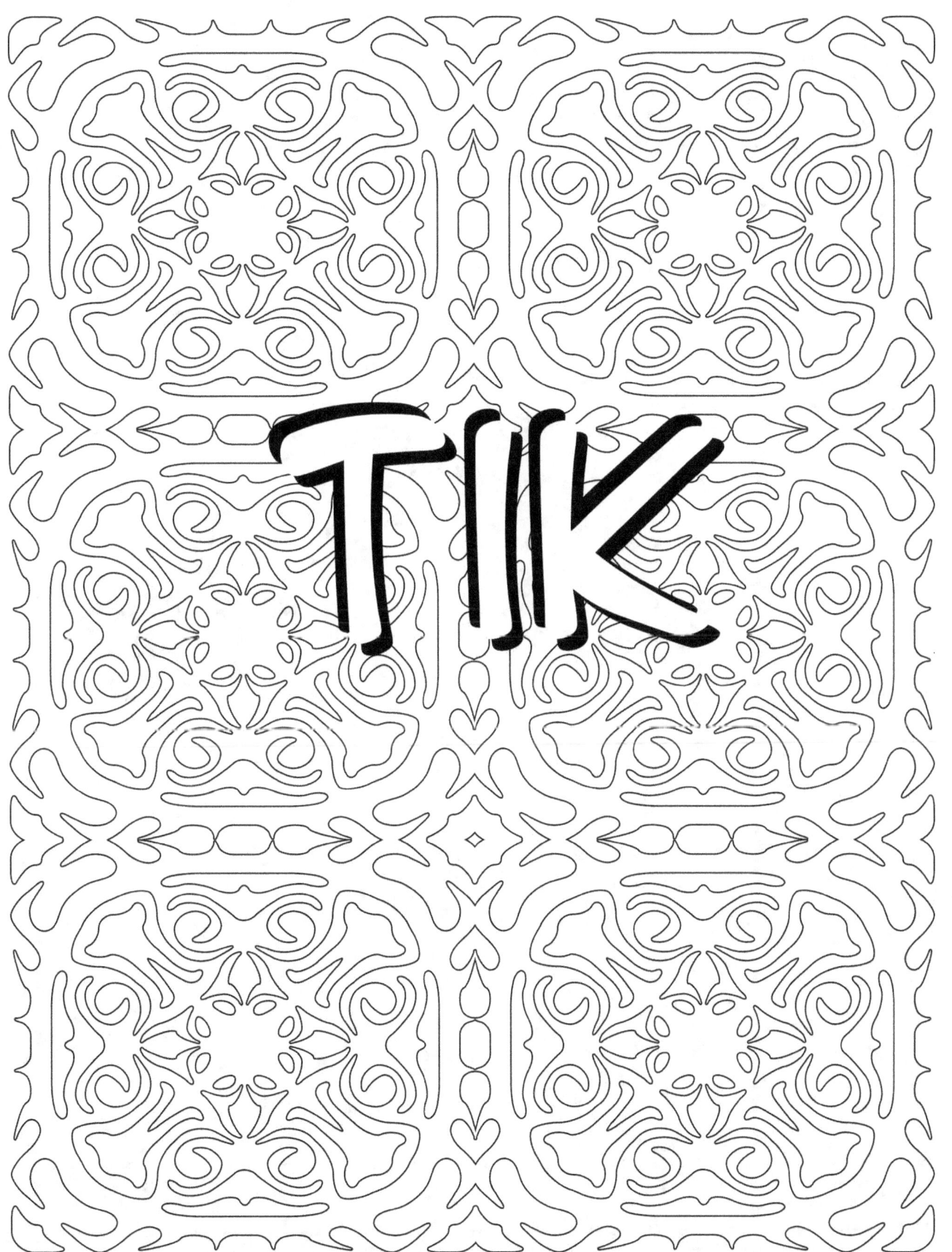

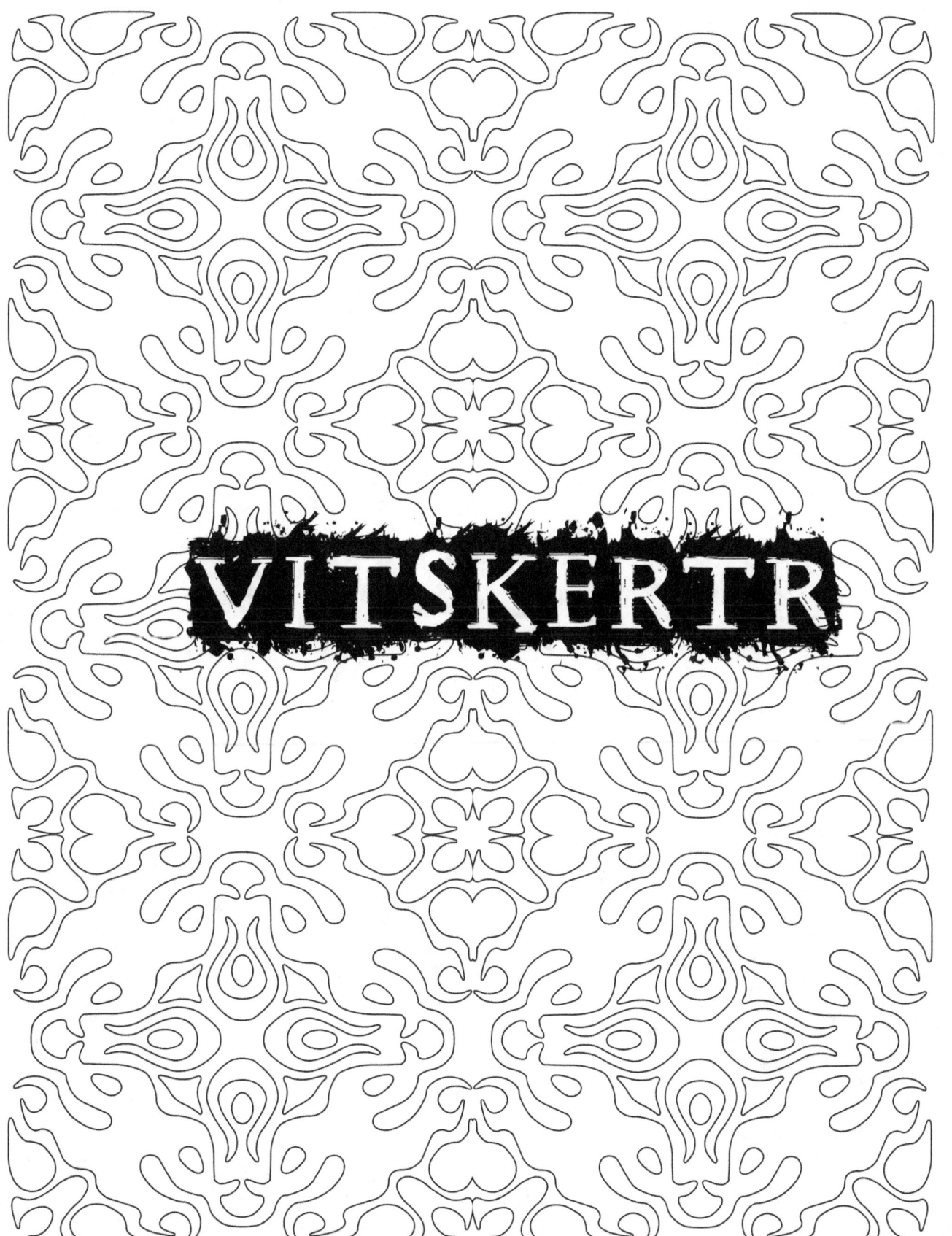

VITSKERTR

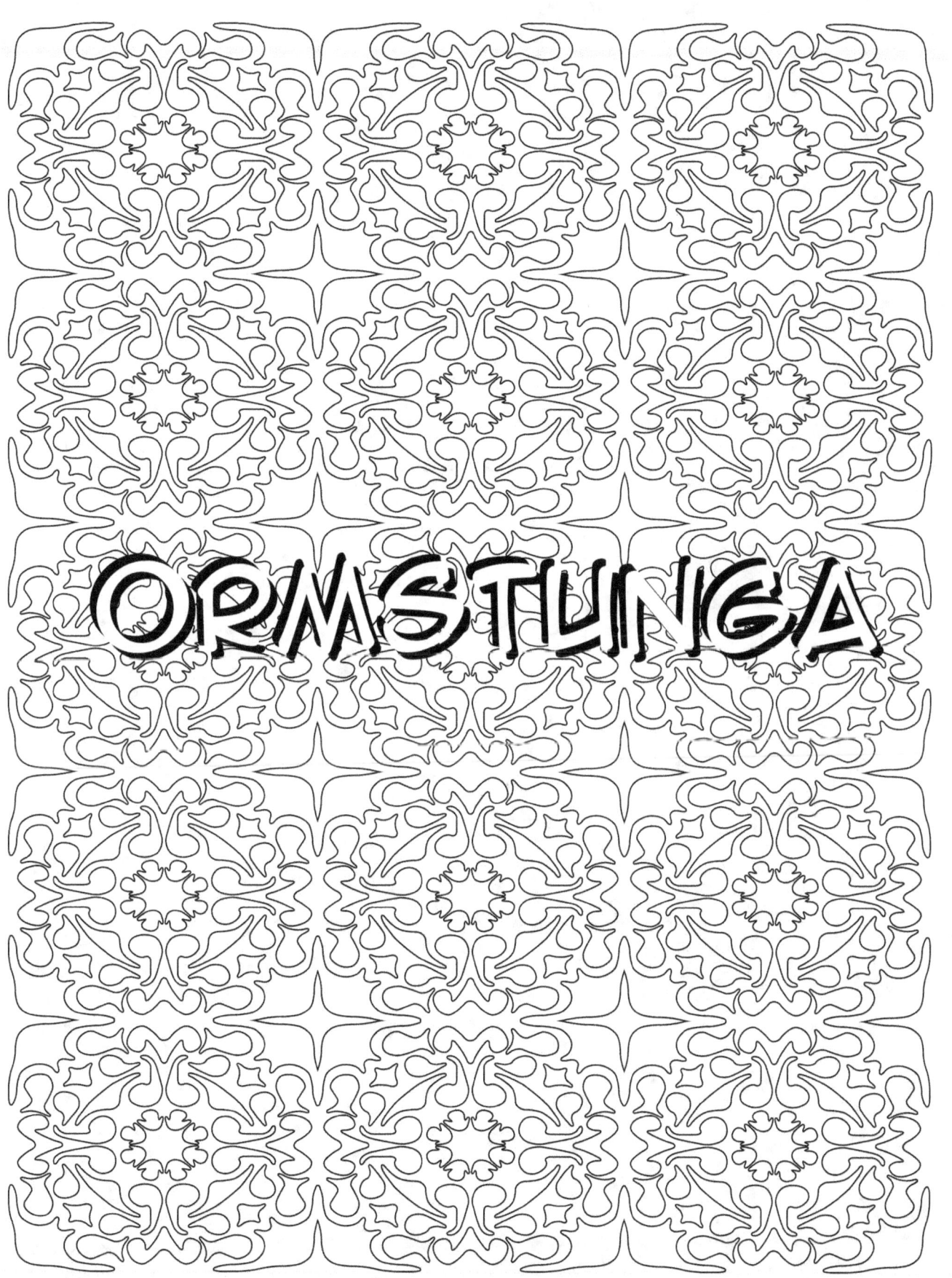

ORMSTUNGA

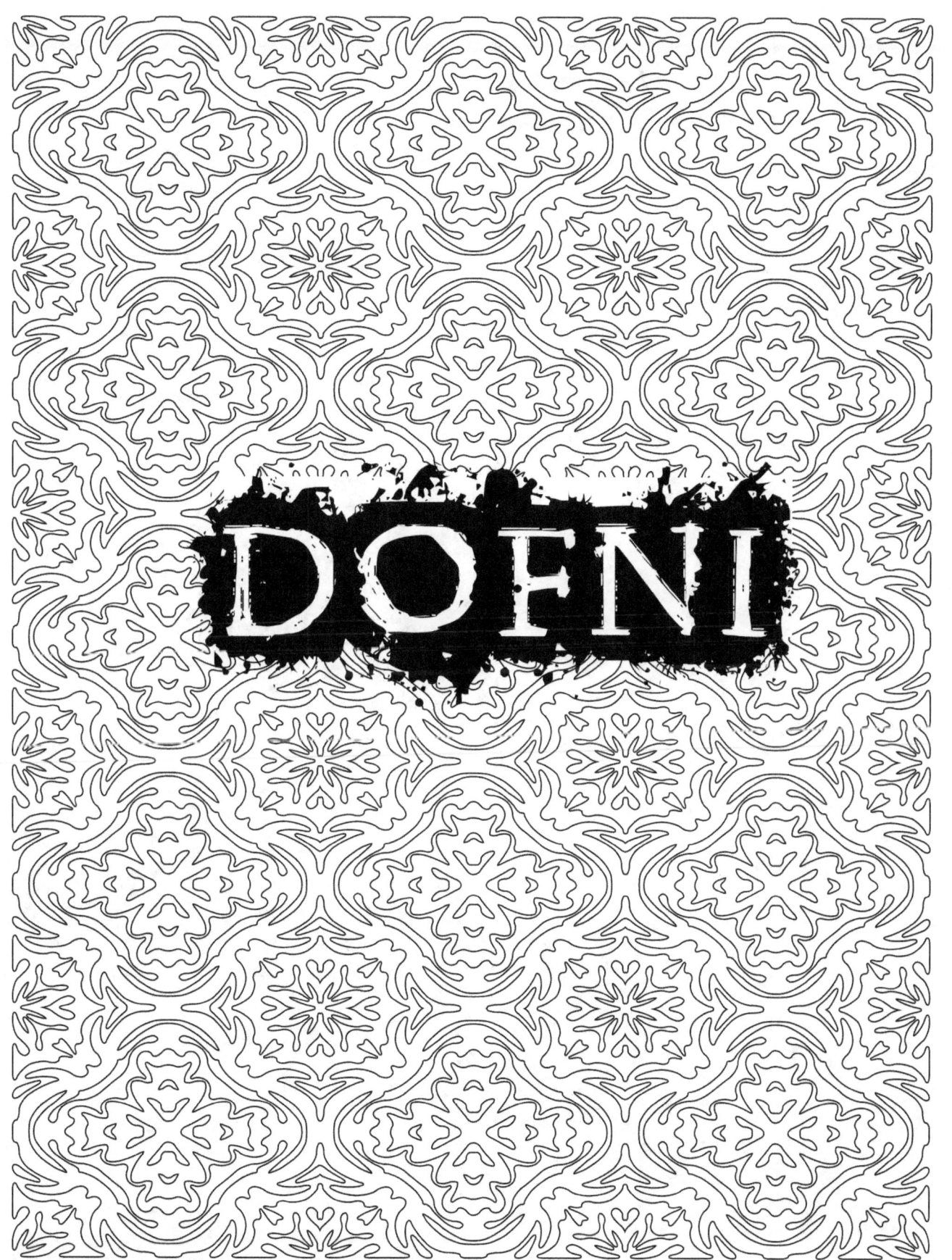

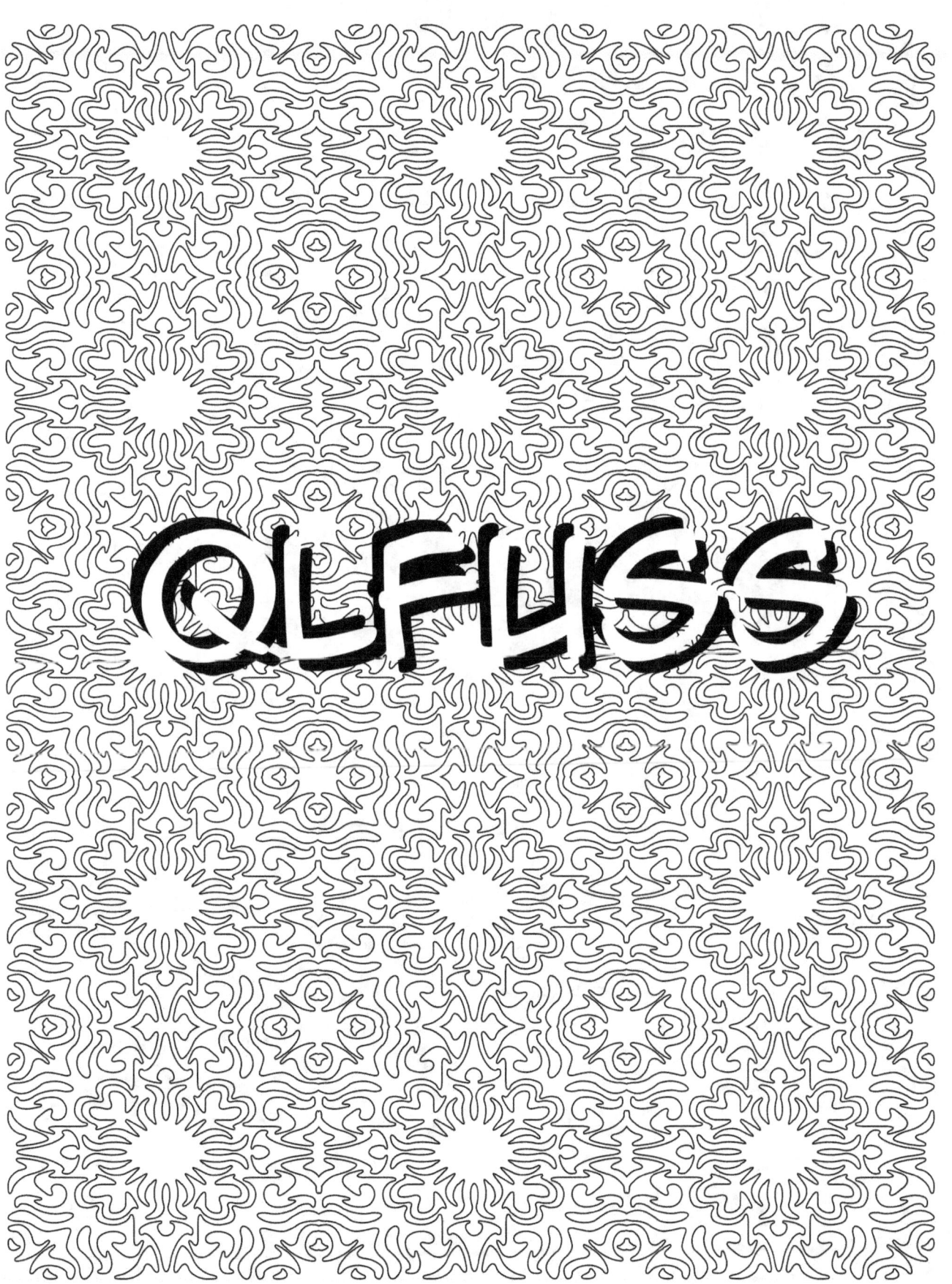

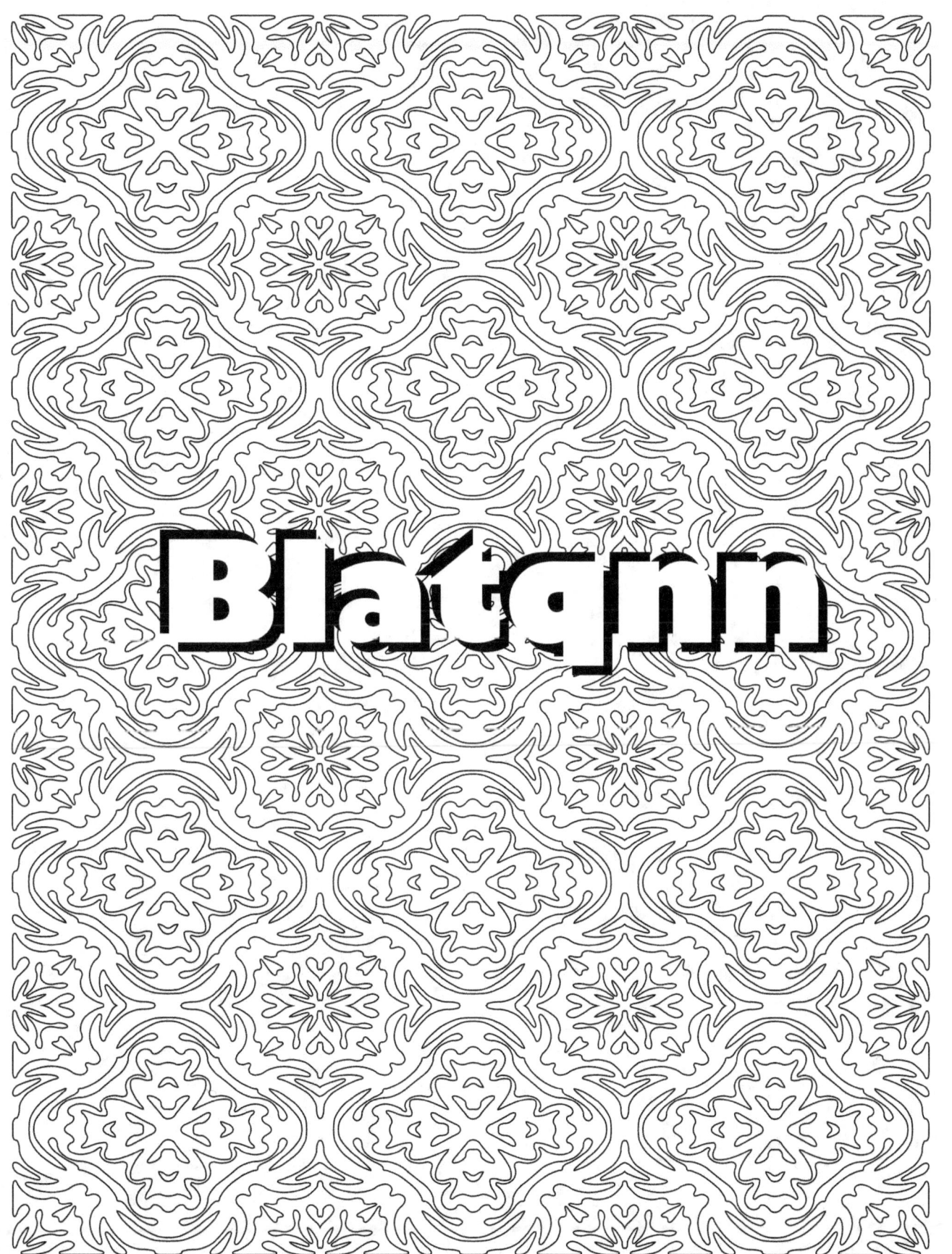

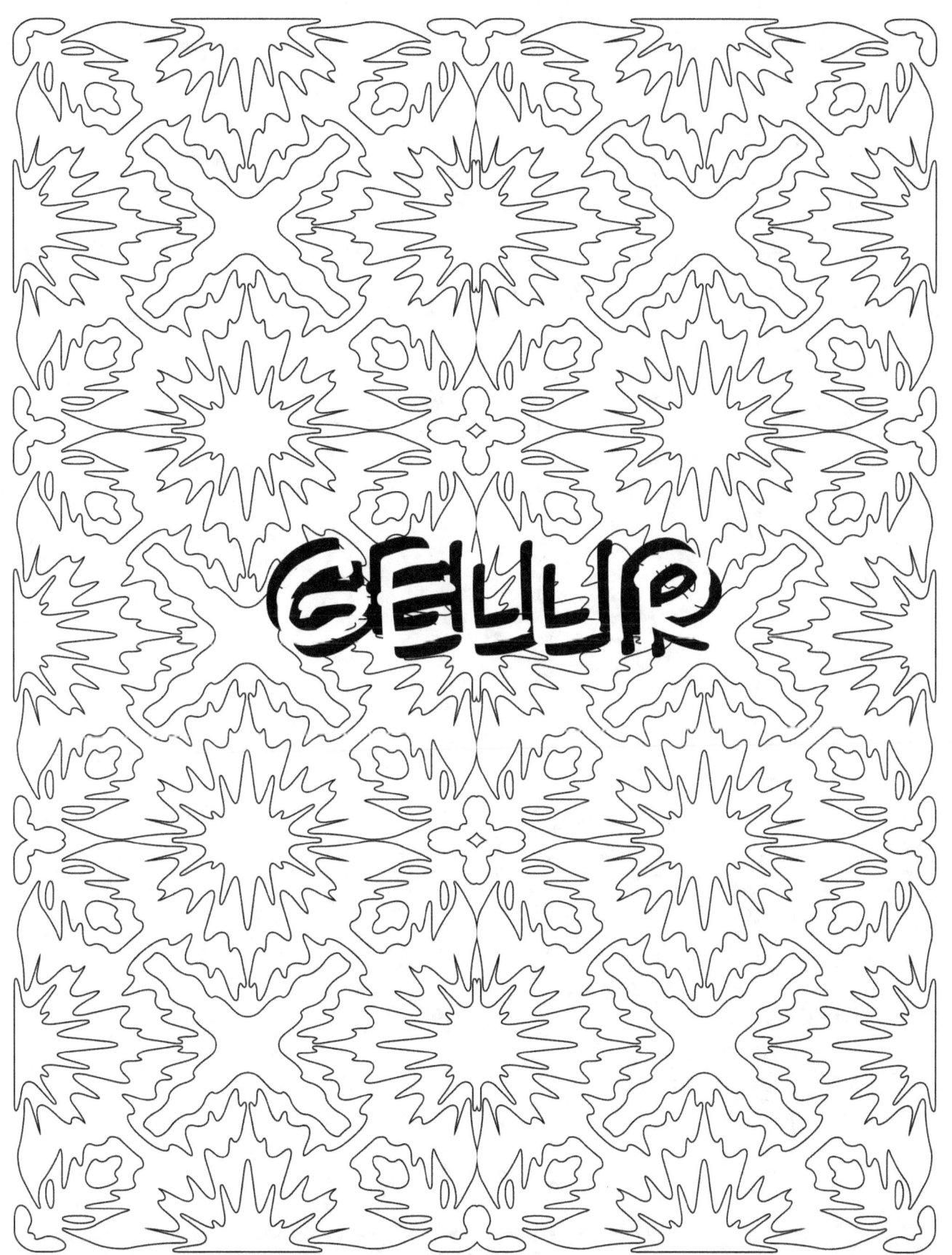

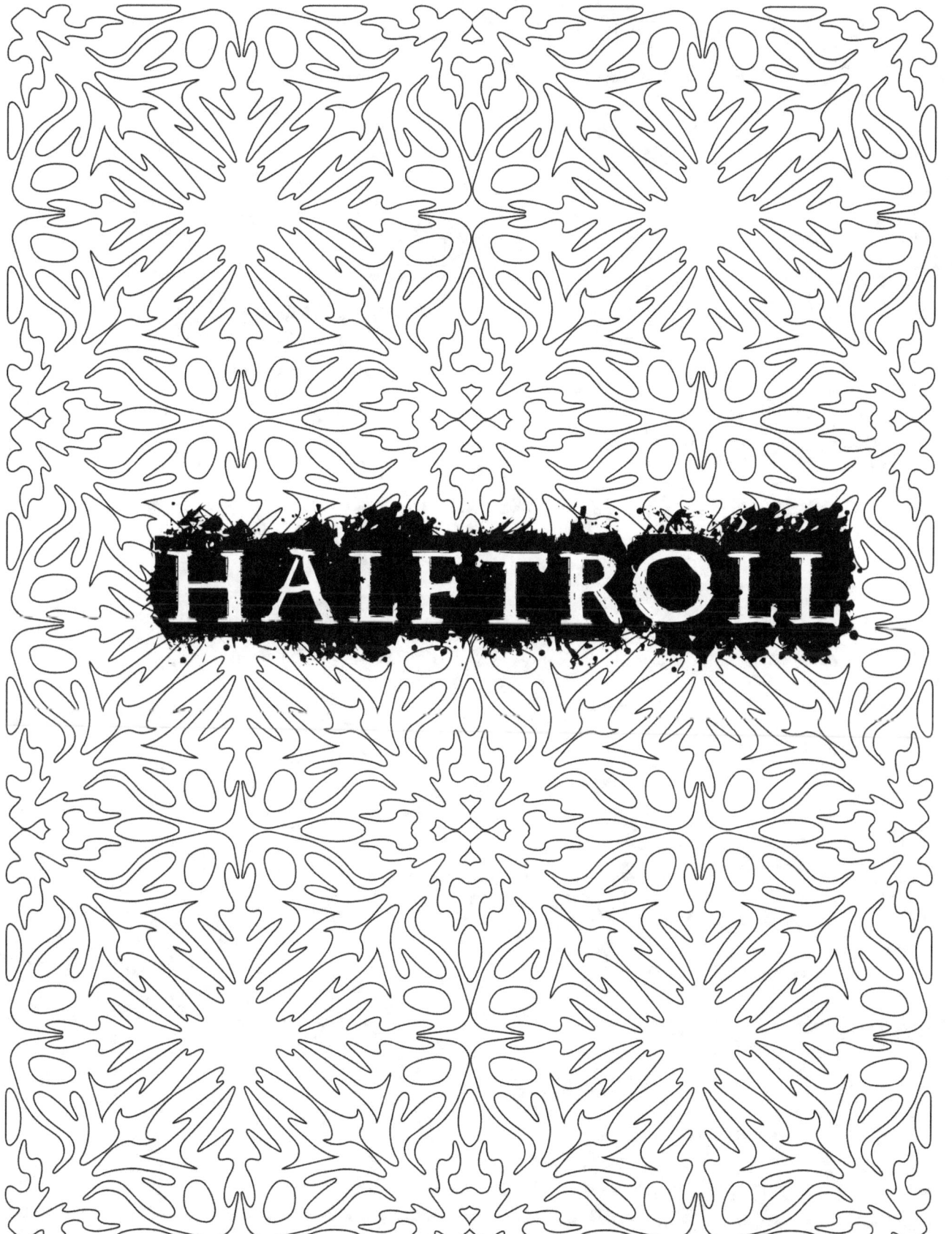

HALFTROLL

Final Words

Now Go Out There And Start Using Those Words!

Have Fun!